THE REVISED EYFS
IN PRACTICE

Thinking, Reflecting and Doing

Ann Langston &
Dr. Jonathan Doherty

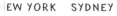

FEATHERSTONE
AN IMPRINT OF BLOOMSBURY
NEW YORK   SYDNEY

Published 2012 by Featherstone Education
An imprint of Bloomsbury Publishing Plc
50 Bedford Square, London, WC1B 3DP

www.bloomsbury.com

ISBN 9781408163948

A CIP record for this publication is available from the British Library.

This book is produced using paper that is made from wood grown in managed, sustainable forests.
It is natural, renewable and recyclable. The logging and manufacturing processes conform to the
environmental regulations of the country of origin.

To see our full range of titles visit www.bloomsbury.com

Acknowledgements
With thanks to Acorn Child Care Limited, Milton Keynes and London Early Years Foundation/
Emli Bendixen for the photographs.
Excerpt from *The Long Term Costs of Numeracy Difficulties*, copyright 2009 Every Child A Chance
Trust, reprinted by kind permission of Every Child A Chance.

Every effort has been made to contact copyright holders of material reproduced in this book.
Any omissions will be rectified in subsequent printings if notice is given to the publishers.

Typeset by Fakenham Prepress Solutions, Fakenham, Norfolk NR21 8NN
Printed and Bound by CPI Group (UK) Ltd, Croydon CR0 4YY

10 9 8 7 6 5 4 3 2

Contents

Introduction

The publication of the *Statutory Framework for the Early Years Foundation Stage* (EYFS) informed by Dame Clare Tickell's independent review of the EYFS: *The Early Years: Foundations for life, health and learning* heralds a new era for early years. From September 2012 this document will set the standards for early learning, development and care for children from birth to five. Unlike the previous EYFS (2007) document with its poster, principles into practice cards, CD-ROM and glossy packaging the revised EYFS is much leaner and less expansive than the earlier version. We believe that new generations of practitioners will find the revised EYFS sparse and more experienced practitioners will question what has changed, so we hope that within this volume these issues will be resolved, or at least addressed in some part.

We are aware though that there are no easy answers and that the greatest challenges are overcome not when we are told what to do but when we develop our own ideas and constantly reflect on our own practice. We have therefore tried to offer opportunities for the reader to stand back and consider practices that are taken for granted alongside introducing what we hope are thought-provoking activities and reflection points. There is rarely time in early years settings for enquiry beyond the here and now: taking the time to reflect will inevitably lead to change since by questioning and challenging our own practices we are likely to arrive at fresh perspectives which will take us in new directions. These ideas will, we hope, inspire the reader to fresh fields of enquiry which we believe will make their journey all the more engaging.

Written in the context of changes to the EYFS this book is organised in three parts.

Part 1 lays the foundation for the book and discusses the changing political, economic and fiscal context that surrounds the revised EYFS framework, before arguing the importance of child development in both policy and practice. Part 2 provides a comprehensive coverage of the learning and development requirements and Part 3 deals with many of the important factors that impact upon children's learning and development throughout the EYFS. Within many chapters boxed Thinking, Reflection and Doing sections provide opportunities for critical engagement with the issues raised. There are also some practical suggestions and small case studies to illuminate theory into practice to enable readers to gain a deeper understanding of the revised EYFS framework.

Part 1 commences with Chapter 1 which considers the background and conditions leading to the revised framework and acknowledges the scale of the sea-change in early years which is likely to impact on practice for many years to come. The importance of starting early and investing in early years is not new; we explore the arguments surrounding this issue, particularly the political dynamic which focuses on investment from an economic standpoint, rather than from a pedagogical perspective. We also address the very topical area of 'school readiness'. We conclude the chapter by returning to the principles upon which early education is based and consider if, how and to what extent these are reflected in the revised framework. Chapter 2 examines the range of typical development for children from pre-birth to five years before focusing on the EYFS as an inclusive framework, which is then explored in the light of legislative changes.

In Part 2 we consider the seven areas of learning and development in the revised EYFS, beginning in Chapter 3 with a rationale for the division of the areas of learning into prime and specific areas and an exploration of how these are inter-connected. In Chapter 4 the three prime areas are explored in depth with reference to their role in children's all-round development. Chapter 5 then goes on to consider the specific areas of learning, focusing on each in depth.

The remaining chapters that comprise Part 3 explore the factors that significantly influence children's learning in the EYFS, beginning in Chapter 6 with an examination of how and why an enabling environment matters for children. Chapter 7 elaborates the connection between play and learning and shows that when practitioners focus on the processes involved in play, positive outcomes are more rather than less achievable. Chapter 8 focuses on the importance of interactions between adults and children. It develops earlier discussions of how relationships build social and emotional skills from an early age, the role of the key person and explores links between well-being, interaction, thinking and learning. Parents, partnerships and home learning matters are discussed in Chapter 9, while in Chapter 10 we examine current research to illustrate how children's learning begins and the many factors that promote it. We then consider the three characteristics of effective learning: playing and exploring; active learning; creativity and critical thinking. The chapter concludes by examining the relationship between teaching and learning and offers some practical strategies to take forward into practice. Finally, in Chapter 11 we draw together pertinent issues which we believe will be important in the future. We also echo and reinforce messages from Cathy Nutbrown's[1] review of early education and childcare qualifications, particularly the recognition that the workforce is fundamental to quality in the early years.

We conclude with a reminder that ultimately we are all responsible for making early education better for young children. We hope that in some small way this book will enthuse and inspire practitioners and remind policy makers of what matters most in the early years.

Ann Langston and Dr. Jonathan Doherty

Policy Matters

Aims of the chapter

- To examine the policy context leading to radical changes in the Early Years Foundation Stage (EYFS) (2012)
- To consider research in relation to the notion of an early 'attainment gap'
- To explore the historical underpinnings of the term 'school readiness'
- To examine the extent to which the EYFS (2012) upholds the principles of the pioneers of early education

It might seem that the last place that government policy matters is in the baby room, pre-school, or classroom where babies and children up to five years of age are cared for and educated, yet it matters a great deal more here than we may have ever imagined. Indeed, through the revised EYFS (2012)[1] government policy continues to direct almost everything in early years education, prescribing: the numbers of adults relative to numbers of children; the amount of space for play; what children should learn when they are cared for out of their own home; as well as the nature of support and guidance that settings should provide for parents and carers. In view of this diverse reach across so many domains of early years education, it is important to understand the context of recent policy direction since we are in the midst of a sea-change which will continue to impact practice in early years settings for many years into the future.

This chapter sets out to explore the policy context which has led to radical changes in the EYFS learning and development requirements, examining why, just two years after the introduction of the EYFS, and with little money left in treasury coffers, a newly-elected coalition government in the UK chose to invest in re-shaping early years education in England. To do so we reflect on changes made to the EYFS (2012)[2] and changing perspectives among the prevailing influences of technology, neuro-science, educational research and economic, and fiscal policy which are determining direction as never before; at the same time we consider the idea of an attainment gap among children from more and less advantaged circumstances and the concept of 'school-readiness' an emerging and contentious issue in England, though one which is well-established in the United States of America. Finally we explore whether and to what extent this new initiative is consistent with the received wisdom highlighted in some well-known principles of early years education.

Background to the EYFS

We start by briefly outlining some of the changes and the background of the EYFS. Recent history of early years education in England shows that when the *Curriculum Guidance for the Foundation Stage*[3] (CGFS) document was introduced in 2000 by the relatively new Labour government, as part of its National Childcare Strategy, it focused on six areas of learning which formed the basis of a curriculum for children aged from three to five years. The success of the CGFS then paved the way for the introduction, in 2003, of a framework for babies and children from birth to three years: *Birth to Three Matters*[4] (BTTM). The BTTM framework was the first national document in England, to focus on the education of this age group. Differences between the two frameworks were fundamental, since the CGFS was based on the idea of 'areas of learning', (transmutable to 'subjects' to be learned) while the BTTM framework took as its starting point the concept of the developing child.

The decision to amalgamate these two documents, together with the *National Standards for Under Eights Daycare and Child Minding*,[5] came shortly after, leading, in 2007, to the introduction of the Early Years Foundation Stage[6] (EYFS). Following the creation of the National Childcare Strategy in 1997, the publication of the CGFS in 2000, and the introduction, in 2003, of the BTTM framework, it became clear that approaches to educating children from birth to five in England were changing radically.

When the idea of the single framework, which subsequently became the EYFS, was proposed, it became clear that while many regarded its introduction as an opportunity, others were concerned about what might be lost in the process. The supporters of the proposed EYFS believed that a joint framework for children from birth to five years of age would ensure that in the future there would be a 'level playing field' for early childhood provision. They belived this would recognise the significant contribution to children's education of all types of providers in the diverse arena of early years, including childminders in their own homes and practitioners in settings as varied as church halls, schools and purpose-built nurseries. Many believed that as a result of this joined-up approach children would benefit greatly and there would

Specific areas: Links to National Curriculum Statutory Programmes of Study
- Literacy: English
- Mathematics: Mathematics
- Understanding the World: a) Science b) Geography c) History d) ICT
- Expressive Arts and Design: a) Art and Design b) Music

Figure 1

be mutual recognition of a shared enterprise by all providers of early education and care. Opposition to the change mainly came from practitioners working with babies and younger children who were anxious about losing the focus on child development which the BTTM framework had brought about. However, there were, and remain, many compelling factors supporting both arguments.

Nevertheless the amalgamation went ahead and the EYFS was successfully implemented in September 2008. Only a short time later, after a comprehensive review, the EYFS has changed again. The greatest of these changes, which will form the focus of much of this book, relate to the separation of the early years curriculum into two parts: the prime areas of learning and the specific, or applied areas of learning. This division is highly significant. Notably it differentiates between child development and 'subject' knowledge, with the prime areas focusing on the developing child, and the specific areas constructed around the knowledge, skills and understanding of areas of learning which are associated with school-type 'subjects', which link into the statutory programmes of study in the National Curriculum for Key Stage 1.

Reflecting on the EYFS (2012), with seven areas of learning and the division into two groups one is perhaps left wondering why this occurred at this particular point in time: whatever reasons are offered it is evident that there has been a major shift in thinking about early education in England. So why have these changes happened?

Influences of technology

One obvious reason is the influence of technology, which is a continual driver of change to our physical, educational and social worlds and which as a result influences our sense of self, our emotions and our learning. Indeed the magnitude of changes in the Industrial Revolution have almost certainly been dwarfed by the emergence of those in recent times created by sophisticated computers which have made possible what our forebears could never dream of. So we live in an age where, through programs like Google Maps (derived from satellite images), new generation phones take us, as virtual travellers, to places around the world, which though not visited can become familiar to us; or consider the speed with which films can be downloaded to a laptop for entertainment, or how, through the use of cutting-edge technology, an adult, unable to walk, is assisted by scientists to complete a 25 mile marathon run.

At the same time, through medical science, non-invasive imaging and scanning techniques have begun to shed light not only on people's health but also on brain functioning, offering enlightenment about for example, atypical cortical features in the brain, responsible for deficits in processing sound which can negatively impact on the development of reading skills in conditions such as dyslexia. Remarkably, it is through discovering these patterns that scientists are able to inform the development of targeted interventions. Interfacing with this is neuroscience: the scientific study of the nervous system.[7] The brain, as we will learn in the next chapter, is like an orchestra made up of many players – recognising each part and its particular contribution to development now seems straightforward because the 'terrain' of the brain has been conquered by scientific exploration – although there is yet still more to learn!

Early childhood research

So, technology is apparent all around us and taken for granted, particularly by the young, who have no reason to imagine a world without it. In an array of new disciplines, brought about because of technological advances, studies of young children are revealing some fascinating findings, as well as providing scientific evidence to prove what was already 'known' at a human level (though not scientifically), as well as throwing into question some earlier misconceptions. So, what does science tell us? One thing that was believed to be true in the past, that has since been proven, is that our emotions influence our learning potential. For example, one study tells us that the elevation of stress hormones, such as cortisol, impair young children's cognitive functioning, particularly memory and learning abilities.[8] This suggests that children who are able to relax and who do not experience stress are likely to gain greater benefit from their experiences. An interesting facet of this is that even where researchers have controlled for IQ and prior attainment, emotional development and other psychosocial factors in the first three years have been shown to '*significantly*

predict academic achievement.[9] This research along with other studies is offering not only proof of previous thinking but also new insights into real-life problems.

At the other end of the learning spectrum, neuroscience has been able to reveal that the plasticity of the brain does not cease during infancy, as was believed previously, because we now know the human brain is just as capable of learning at 60 as it is at six years of age. However, we also know that the brain is likely to learn some things more effectively at certain stages than others. So, for example in language learning, it is now known it is easier to learn the grammar of a language sooner, rather than later, while when it comes to vocabulary there are no time limits on learning new words. This conclusion is based on findings which show that different brain areas contribute to processing language and that the part of the brain which processes the semantic information in words such as 'cat', 'house' or 'car' is different from the part activated when words which provide grammatical information such as 'up', 'of' and 'from' are used.[10] Furthermore, in relation to the acquisition of speech sounds, it is known that initially newborns have the potential to learn the sounds of any language, yet as the brain connects with familiar sounds from the native language, sensitivity to a non-native language is lost. Studies such as these make compelling arguments towards the 'early is better' view for young children's learning, though there are those who warn that what is perceived as a loss of brain cells (synaptic pruning) may show that greater, not less, learning is taking place. This is because the brain is making an effort to ensure that the important connections related to native language are being laid down so that it does not waste effort on something that is not functional to the child's early speech and language development.[11] However, there are many persuasive arguments supporting the case that 'early is better' where children's learning is concerned.

We will shortly go on to consider some of the 'unproven' but powerful ideas of the pioneers of early education since these are representative of the views which although not proven by science have made sense for decades to many early educators and on which the principles of the EYFS are primarily founded.

Economic and fiscal policy

Based on many findings about human learning the attention of economists has been drawn to early education as a fertile area with the potential to right many of the woes associated with the 'costs' to society of non-working families on 'welfare' (in the US) and those who rely on the state to meet their material needs in this country. Many findings indicate that among the workless (and the prison population) low levels of literacy and numeracy are factors that negatively influence lives and work prospects, which then impact on an individual's ability to function in a literate society this in turn leads to marginalisation of the individual and to other conditions such as depression, mental illness, homelessness and so on.

Economists, wanting to change this bleak picture, argue that by starting early we can prevent poor children becoming poor adults.[12] This is an argument which sees early childhood education as an economic investment; it is not new, the same agenda was espoused in the 1960's through the Head Start programme for three and four year old children in the US as part of President Johnson's 'War on Poverty': '*The goal of the program was to bring poor children up to the level of their more advantaged peers by the time they reached school entry. Head Start was to do this by providing a broad array of services, including medical screenings, nutritious meals and parent training in addition to early childhood education*.'[13] Indeed, the success of this programme has been heralded by many including, as one would expect, the National Head Start Association which reminds educators, economists and politicians alike of the high return on investment, since, for every one dollar spent, it is estimated that between seven and nine dollars is saved. It is because of this return that we are told '*Investing in early childhood education programs, such as Head Start, yields a higher rate of return to society than spending money on secondary education and job training programs*.'[14]

Comparisons between the Head Start programme and the Sure Start programme in this country are obvious. The Sure Start programme also grew from recognition of the need to support children and families so that parents could be taken out of poverty and into work. Brought about in 1997/98 as part of the Labour government's comprehensive spending review, Sure Start was set up under Norman Glass, a civil servant working in the Treasury. While it is known he wanted value for money he is reputed to have *'worked hard to ensure that the programme was based not only on good research evidence, but was also underpinned by core values; it had to be not only cost effective, but socially just to ensure that children had the best possible start in life'.*[15] Massive investment followed, culminating in the setting up of 3,000 Sure Start Centres, as well as the development of the concept of funded early education. This was initially through vouchers, introduced in England and Wales in April 1997, which entitled parents to £1,100 towards the cost of three terms of pre-school education in the state or private sector, and *'later discontinued by the new Labour government in summer 1997 and the resources set aside for its operation, amounting to £674m, were diverted into the development of early years education'.*[16] In the last decade or so this led to the provision of free places for up to a maximum of 15 hours a week for 38 weeks a year for all three and four year olds. The offer of free early education has recently been extended to 40% of the most disadvantaged two year olds. In addition, associated services and provision, including Early Excellence Centres, Sure Start programmes, and finally Children's Centres were also given targets to achieve in relation to the numbers of families who they supported. This included getting one parent into employment, mothers who successfully attended smoking cessation programmes, mothers who breast-fed their child, or accompanied their children to stay and play sessions, or who attended skills training and/or educational courses. The benefits of these have been reported as variable for a number of reasons, though many will have had a positive effect on individuals; however it is beyond the scope of this book to consider them further here, though they are undoubtedly important. In order to judge the success of this significant investment in early years education, the EYFS Profile (EYFSP)[17] was put in place, to measure the outcomes for young children, using this as a proxy measure of impact.

The EYFSP

What did the EYFSP show? It revealed that across all the scales (measures) of the EYFSP, including language, social development, knowledge and understanding of the world and physical development, there was a year on year improvement[18] from 2007 through to 2011. However, the performance of boys lagged behind outcomes for girls and summer born children tended to do less well than their autumn born peers.[19] It showed too that some children did less well especially those from lower income families and some children for whom English was an additional language (EAL), though other data show that achievements of children in the latter group often compare well with their peers at a slightly later stage.

Attainment gap

The difference in outcomes between children from more and less advantaged families became a concern to policy makers who described it as an 'attainment gap'; known to be established very early and difficult to influence. The idea of an attainment gap was first mooted in the UK following research on young children's cognitive skills. These related to findings on children's performance at 22 months in laboratory tests where children were assessed in cube stacking, language use, personal development and drawing; and at 42 months on their performance in counting, speaking and copying different designs. This research showed: *'those in the bottom quartile at 22 months are significantly more likely to get no qualifications than children in the top quartile and significantly less likely to get 'A' levels or higher qualifications. For the top and bottom SES [Socio-economic status] groups, differences at 42 months strongly predict final educational qualifications. So, in combination with the SES factor, the pre-school scores still matter'.*[20] In spite of many questions raised by this research it has been argued in defence of these findings: *'the longer-term outcomes of the children in the original study appear to back up Feinstein's deeply held view that the potential of the least privileged in society is routinely squandered'.*[21] Subsequently research studies have continued to uphold these findings and a myriad of reports have highlighted the importance of cognitive and social development, together with family background and parental behaviour as being influential for children's life chances.[22] [23] [24] In one sense this plethora of literature has had the capacity to bind the politics of left and right in this country, since a number of influential reports were published at a pivotal point politically, coinciding with a general election after 13 years of Labour rule.

The change from a Labour government to a Conservative-led coalition in May 2011, briefly stopped the world of early education in its tracks, uncertain about what a new government of the centre right would prioritise. It had signalled that funds were low, swingeing cuts would be the order of the day and a downturn in the economy would follow meaning funding would become more scarce. A universal sigh of relief followed when Children's Minister, Sarah Teather, led the coalition's policy in early years, announcing her government's Vision for Early Years, which indicated: *The Government knows that high quality health services, early education, and care for young children and their families make a real difference.*[25] Sometime later a website and a joint department of health and education initiative targeted family support,[26] outlining a focus on, among other things, child development and readiness for school, a slimmer EYFS, the importance of early intervention and of supporting parents and more recently the suggestion of funded parenting classes – all in order to influence children's learning.

Many policy makers acknowledge the importance of early education, if for very different reasons; we will shortly consider the views of early educationalists. The fact that successive governments recognize the undeniable link between health, affluence (and lack of it) and early education has been welcomed by many though, as with all things, there are sceptics who either suspect or question such a rationale. Fuelling the debate further is the contribution of an unlikely advocate of early education, James Heckman,[27] Professor of Economics at the University of Chicago, whose voice is heeded here and in the US. Heckman, with other economists such as Robert Lynch[28] calls for early investment on the basis that *'early success begets later success',*[29] reiterating the links between poverty, health, life chances, employment and well-being. This is summed up in a presentation given by Heckman to the Young Foundation in which he argued that social-emotional skills and good health lead to improvements in cognition which in turn leads to *'increased productivity, higher income, better health, more family investment, upward mobility and reduced social costs'*[30] – one is left with the question 'what is there not to like?' a question we will explore in the next section.

The concept of 'school-readiness'

Many of these discussions may seem to be far away from the reality of a revised EYFS in September 2012. Yet if we consider the lessons from the US, particularly from Heckman and others, it becomes clear that economists, who have been open about their reasons for being interested in early education, believe that continued investment in early education must yield long term economic returns, (on the basis these reduce welfare payments and increase productivity). There is therefore a desire to institute a new measure for judging the effectiveness of the 'intervention', also known as early education, in effect what has become known as the 'school readiness' debate. This term found its way into the EYFS for the first time when the draft EYFS statutory framework[31] was published in July 2011. So what is school readiness, why is it being talked about and will it cut across the principles of the EYFS?

The Head Start programme in the US, followed by the Santa Rosa District School System, identifies three essential domains which it is suggested affect school readiness: early education, mental health and disabilities and health and nutrition. This focus is very similar to the one described earlier, in relation to Sure Start, although as also indicated earlier, the term 'school readiness' did not previously occur as such in the associated UK literature. While this appears to be an accepted outcome for early education in the US the same response has not been seen here, for several reasons. Firstly because there was no national debate in this country about the term and secondly when it did appear it seemed to suggest that children's experiences in their earliest years were merely preparation

for later, stating: *'Teaching in the early years should be focused on improving children's 'school readiness', guiding the development of children's (cognitive, behavioural, physical and emotional) capabilities, so that children can take full advantage of the learning opportunities presented to them in school.*[32] Some of the heat was taken out of this debate with the government response to feedback on the draft EYFS, which indicated that the term had not been well received by *'a significant minority'* which has since led to clarification in the EYFS 2012 that school readiness refers to readiness for Year 1; the year after children start school in reception classes in England.

In the EYFS 2012, we are informed 'school readiness': *'refers to children having the broad range of essential knowledge and skills that provide the right foundation for future progress, through school and life'.*[33] The problem with this definition is that it lacks conviction and has failed to engage either practitioners or influencers in the real discussions that might have convinced those who oppose it. Acknowledgement of the UNICEF definition of 'school readiness' which relates to three domains might have been more convincing (these are the child, the school and the family). UNICEF's arguments in its defence are:

- 'Children's readiness for school focuses on learning and developmental outcomes.

- Schools' readiness for children focuses on school-level outcomes and practices that foster every child's smooth transition into primary school and advance all children's learning.
- Families' readiness for school focuses on the attitudes of parents, caregivers and older siblings, and their involvement in children's early learning and development and transition to school'.[34]

It concludes by noting: '*These three dimensions work synergistically to promote or curtail school readiness. A child who is ready for school has basic skills and knowledge in multiple areas.*'[35] So, the question remains whether early education should only focus on the present or whether it should hold the expectation that what happens in the earliest years is important for children's future lives and life chances. Probably neither of these positions represents the views of either the minority who challenge the concept of school readiness, nor of its champions.

Principles of early education

To offer a perspective on the purpose of early education we will briefly consider, some common principles of the pioneers of early education, discussed by Bruce,[36] since it is on these that the four principles of the original EYFS (2007) were based: a unique child, positive relationships, an enabling environment and learning and development. We will now attempt to assess the extent to which the revised EYFS (2012) accords with the pioneering principles, although only four of the ten principles have been selected because of their direct relevance to the purposes of early education.

The first principle we consider is: '*Childhood is seen as valid in itself, as part of life and not simply as preparation for adulthood. Thus education is seen similarly as something of the present and not just preparation and training for later*'.[37] Clearly this first principle is not supported in the EYFS (2012) – because of the espousal by the government of an instrumental view of education which is based on a cost-benefit analysis. However this raises the question of whether the ends are justifiable: if they are then perhaps this principle is challenged to remain in its present form. If not, then the problem remains, of the gap, which widens as children grow older and which marks out some children for success and others for failure, though, as always there are children who succeed against the odds.[38]

A second principle for consideration in this debate is: '*Learning is not compartmentalised, for everything links*', this is much more in tune with the school readiness approach since it appears to suggest that all learning is connected and that 'subjects' of the curriculum should not be split, as they are at other stages of schooling. This is certainly a tenet of the 'school readiness' view since there is recognition of the influence of affect on cognition, which is that learning in one domain is heavily predicated on development in others. Indeed this is further supported since we know that '*experts in the field*

of neurobiology and education now view learning as a multifaceted exchange between cognitive, emotional and physiological elements'.[39] Some might argue that the division of areas of learning in the EYFS, referred to earlier, is the opposite of this, since it has separated the prime areas from the specific areas, on the basis that development in the prime areas is functional to development in the specific areas. However, others would argue that by initially focusing on these areas of development children are much more likely to succeed subsequently.

The third principle we explore could also be seen to align with the school readiness debate in that it states: '*The whole child is considered to be important. Health, physical and mental, is emphasised, as well as the importance of feelings and thinking, and spiritual aspects*'. Clearly, school readiness discussions do support this position since it is argued in the literature: '*School readiness is more than academics: practices that also consider children's physical, social and emotional progress will be most effective in supporting school readiness*'.[40] A position statement by a leading early childhood organisation argued though that: '*the commitment to promoting universal school readiness requires: addressing the inequities in early life experience so that all children have access to the opportunities that promote school success.*' Concluding: '*The traditional construct of readiness unduly places the burden of proof on the child. Until the inequities of life experience are addressed, the use of readiness criteria for determining school entry or placement blames children for their lack of opportunity .... [and that] it is the responsibility of schools to meet children's needs as they enter school*'.[41] This is a view with which many would concur.

This leads us to the last principle to be examined, which states: '*There are specially receptive periods of learning at different stages of development.*' Without doubt this principle is an example of what was discussed at the beginning of this chapter with reference to beliefs, which had no scientific basis, but which have been shown to be true as a result of scientific advances. Returning to this discussion it is clear that there are periods in children's lives when learning can be more successful if these occur earlier, rather than later. So, for example we have established that while some aspects of language learning are likely to be more successful if they occur earlier there are also other skills that could be learned later: such as typing on a keyboard. So, it is possible that through separating the EYFS into the prime and specific areas the EYFS (2012) supports this belief, since it emphasises the areas that are more important for children's development at particular stages, the prime areas initially and the specific areas subsequently.

In conclusion of this discussion there are many aspects of the revised EYFS, which contrary to expectation could be said to support some of the principles of early education. The question remains whether by relinquishing the first principle in favour of an instrumental approach to early education the outcomes for children will be worthwhile, increasing their life chances in the ways envisioned by successive governments here and in the US.

Conclusion

It would seem, on balance that the radical changes to the EYFS would probably have occurred whichever political party was in power in the UK when 2011 began because there had always been a commitment to its review two years on from publication. The incoming coalition government could have deferred the review given the lack of funding available, yet it chose to reform the relatively newly established, successful EYFS framework. This was in spite of more than 70% of respondents agreeing they favoured it and Dame Clare Tickell, its reviewer, noting that two years on *'the EYFS ...... has played a crucial role in contributing to a system that has indeed received international recognition and plaudits'.*[42] So why were changes made to the EYFS?

Changes were made to the EYFS for the following reasons:

- Election of a new UK government coincided with the timing of the proposed review of the EYFS.
- Recognition that children's life chances could be influenced positively – thus offering the possibility of counteracting vast-ranging social, economic, health and other influences known to create and/or contribute to an attainment gap.

- An awareness of lessons being learned in the US from Head Start and other programmes which revealed convincing evidence to support the value of intervening early in children's lives to prevent failure later.
- A recognition that these factors could be impacted through supporting families so that their children's health and well-being was optimised and that ultimately they would be able to benefit from their early education.
- Increasing technological developments allowed neuroscience to reveal more about the brain and how different parts of the brain work including, for example, that stress can negatively impact learning capacity. Findings from this area have been and will continue to be powerful in informing debates about the importance of the first three years in children's lives and in relation to the potential impact these can have over time.[43][44]
- Finally, and something of an unexpected contribution, are the lessons from economists who while arguing the economic case nonetheless support the view (whatever their personal motives) that investment in early years education makes sense.

It would seem that if we are to change children's life chances there are many ways to do this: the easiest, and possibly the most effective way is to fund universal early years education. This step has been taken in this country for all three and four year olds; we are on our way to extend this, through the offer to 40% of the most disadvantaged two year olds. Work to support families is continuing to develop from the local Sure Start programmes begun in the 1990s through the Children's Centres of today. What is being offered is not without flaws, yet we have come a long way from the 1990's when free education for pre-schoolers was referred to as a 'patchwork' of provision. The patchwork has been strengthened, the need has been recognised but what must not be lost are children's *'rights to develop their personality, talents and mental and physical abilities to their fullest potential, to play and to be educated.*[45]

The ramifications of the changes in the EYFS (2012) will be many and some will be welcomed more than others. A focus on communication and language, personal, social and emotional development and physical development with the youngest children is likely to receive a very positive press. Inevitably this will need to extend from the setting into the home since interventions with the child alone are insufficient; this will require practitioners to be skilful in working with adults as well as children, which will make greater demands on a workforce which is predominantly female and low-paid. At the point of writing this book the Interim Report of the

Nutbrown Review[46] indicates the following broad areas of agreement across the sector in relation to the early years workforce:

- 'Qualifications need to be of a consistently high quality to give employers confidence
- Qualifications need to reflect the EYFS, and make early years staff confident to work within it
- An understanding of child development – particularly for the earliest age group (birth to seven) – is essential
- We have different expectations of what people should know at different levels of education. Level 2 will be more generic, whereas level 3 and above should provide specialist knowledge and expertise
- The sector craves a more professional status and ethos, reflecting the best practice that is already evident
- There is no single 'one size fits all' approach to qualifications
- The Early Years Professional Status has improved practice, but there are still issues around parity with Qualified Teacher Status
- Learning is lifelong – and the qualification journey should not end with the first qualification. Opportunities for progression are important, as are ongoing professional development experiences for all early years workers, so that career development and Continuing Professional Development (CPD) are expectations of all members of the workforce.'[47]

The outcomes of this review will signal another new direction in early years – this illustrates exactly our point at the start of this chapter that government policy matters in the early years! We will now consider child development.

Development Matters

Aims of the chapter

- To consider the range of typical development from pre-birth to five years
- To question and challenge linear conceptions of development
- To explore the EYFS as an inclusive framework for all children
- To reinforce the importance of laying good foundations in early years to reduce inequalities and improve the life chances of children

This chapter sets out to confirm the importance of child development in the revised EYFS Statutory Framework (2012) which makes reference to the accompanying *Development Matters*[1] non-statutory guidance material to explore its use in practice. We begin by clarifying what is meant by development and argue that a child's individual development should not be viewed as a linear pathway, but more as a 'flow of constant change', occurring in many directions and at different speeds of change. The chapter then goes on to reinforce the uniqueness of development with reference to psychologist Urie Bronfenbrenner, founder of the Head Start programme in the USA's ecological model which describes the contexts that help to shape individual development. We then explore the EYFS as an inclusive framework in which all children, including those with Special Educational Needs (SEN), can flourish. The chapter moves to conclusion by reinforcing the case for firm foundations to be laid in the early years that may redress broader societal, academic and health inequalities.

The wonder that is child development

For years we have been intrigued by human development. Early years practitioners working with young children, have the privilege of observing children first hand and seeing their development unfold daily. Parents recall milestones in their children's development with pride and uncanny accuracy. What happens in the early years is crucial to the developmental trajectory of children. The aspects of development are essential building blocks for learning and development in children's present lives and vital for their future life chances. Dame Claire Tickell's opening words in the response to the Minister of State for Children and Families in the EYFS Review[2] clearly underscore how important child development is:

'The earliest years in a child's life are absolutely critical. There is overwhelming international evidence that foundations are laid in the first years of life which, if weak, can have a permanent and detrimental impact on children's longer term development. A child's future choices, attainment, wellbeing, happiness and resilience are profoundly affected by the quality of the guidance, love and care they receive during these first years.'

These words are a welcome reminder of the significance of child development and why it should hold a central place in policy documents and professional literature pertaining to young children. Knowing how children develop in their formative years is crucial so that practitioners, teachers and parents are able to meet the individual cognitive, social, emotional, language and physical needs of young children at home, in schools and in settings.

What do we understand by the term 'child development'? Essentially, development is about the changes that take place over time, changes that begin in the womb, continue during the post-natal period and into the early childhood years and beyond.

It is now generally understood that development does not proceed in a linear path and we know from research that children follow pathways that are far from linear, developing at times quickly in one aspect and less quickly in another. The analogy of a river may be useful here, winding this way and that, sometimes slow, then quickly, opening up smaller tributaries from time to time but all the while leading on with a clear direction. Each child develops at his or her own pace, although there are periods of obvious transition in development, as one 'stage' leads into the next one. What is to be protected is the intrinsic value of each and every stage of a child's development journey. It is important not to rush or attempt to hothouse children's development, but rather recognise and support each developmental phase.

Developmental stages

This being said, it is common to talk about the prenatal stage (from conception to birth) infancy to toddlerhood (up to two years) and the early childhood stage (from two to five years) and to describe the many milestones associated with typical development at these ages. Let us briefly now take a closer look at development at each of these traditionally described stages.

1 The first stage reflects incredible change as the foetus grows in the safety of the mother's womb over the 38 weeks of the gestation period. By four weeks a heartbeat is established, limbs appear as buds and the head, ears and eyes are evident. By 12 weeks, all major body organs are formed. By 16 weeks the cerebrum area of the brain has expanded and skin appears over the body as a thin translucent layer. By 28 weeks, organs are maturing, kidneys function and from now on the foetus is ready for birth, equipped for survival in the world to come outside the womb.

2 The infancy to toddler stage sees further changes in physical appearance and development in cognitive and perceptual capacity, and in relationships with others. There is an explosion in oral language. By three months a child smiles back when smiled at by another person and by six months is able to recognise a familiar face. By 12 months many children can stand up without assistance and will say their first word. By 18 months most children will be walking and able to say around eight to ten words that others can understand. By the time they are two years old, typical vocabulary is around 200 words; they can feed themselves with a spoon and refer to themselves using 'me' and 'mine'. They are developing their own unique personalities, are active explorers of their immediate environments and can comfort others who are in distress.

3 In early childhood, we see a refinement of many physical skills, advances in emotional control and increased skill with verbal language and language structures. By the age of five a child's height is double their length at birth; their bones are stronger and their body shape more mature. Their unique self is becoming established and their ability to make friends with peers and play with other children has increased. Many children know basic colours, many know some letters of the alphabet and some can make sentences of up to six words. They

enjoy mark-making, listening to stories, singing, counting and are showing more proficiency in fundamental movement skills like running, jumping, skipping and hopping. Such is the pace and the wonder of early development!

Child development in the EYFS

The EYFS (2012)[3] places the prime areas of Personal, Social and Emotional Development, Communication and Language and Physical Development at the beginning of the developmental journey for children because of their particular importance, and we address the detail of these areas in later chapters. The EYFS indicates that these areas are *'crucial for igniting children's curiosity and enthusiasm for learning, and for building their capacity to learn, form relationships and thrive'*[4] Babies are primed to understand their environment by relating to and communicating with others and engaging physically in their experiences in an integrated and inter-related way. Of course, personal, social, and emotional development, physical development, and communication and language development are closely linked to one another and are central to all other areas of learning and development.

As in many documents, child development has been compartmentalised into domains in the Statutory Framework, and in Development Matters, into broad stages. However, we need to be mindful of the holistic nature and interconnectedness of child development, and readers should think of development as a flow of constant change, viewing it in a holistic way as a journey that each child undertakes. The final destination for each child can be similar, but the paths taken along the way are unique.

Development Matters in the Early Years Foundation Stage (EYFS),[5] is non-statutory guidance which accompanies the revised EYFS (2012) and replaces the previous Practice Guidance. This revised Development Matters guidance refers to the four themes of the revised EYFS framework and how the principles that inform them work together to support young children. It offers pointers to development related to six stages of typical development: birth–11 months; 8–20 months; 16–26 months; 22–36 months; 30–50 months and 40–60+ months. These overlapping bands have been retained from the 2007 version of the EYFS, and the guidance is intended to help parents and practitioners to identify each child's individual development pathway from birth to five.

As a document it has both strengths and weaknesses. It separates development into age bands which practitioners may find helpful, although the descriptors in each age band are, as previously, fairly broad. The excellent material from Early Support which supplemented the earlier version has not been provided which will mean that those looking for more detailed information on child development will need to turn elsewhere. Thus, as a stand-alone document, it could be considered insufficient in its present form since it provides only a very brief exploration of child development. However the provision of a 'what adults could do' column in Positive Relationships and 'what adults could provide' in Enabling Environments to support practitioners, is much more detailed and helpful.

The Development Matters guidance is also intended to be used in daily planning, observation and assessment. Practitioners are encouraged to observe the child in a variety of planned and unplanned activities and contexts, reflecting their discussions with parents about the child's experiences and behaviours at home. By observing what a child can do and referring to the examples of typical development in the A Unique Child columns, practitioners can make decisions about the child's present development and the next steps for their learning. Practitioners are invited to use the guidance in the columns Positive Relationships and Enabling Environments as starting points to decide how to best support learning and development and provide next steps.

Using the EYFS

To illustrate this, let us turn to the descriptions from Development Matters in Communication and Language/Listening and Attention/16–26 months.

A Unique Child/Observing what a child is learning

- Listens to and enjoys rhythmic patterns in rhymes and stories.
- Enjoys rhymes and demonstrates listening by trying to join in with actions or vocalisations.
- Rigid attention – may appear not to hear.

The Positive Relationships/What adults could do

- Encourage young children to explore and imitate sound.
- Talk about the different sounds they hear, such as a tractor's 'chug chug' while sharing a book.

Further support is provided in the column Enabling Environments/What adults could provide

- Collect resources that children can listen to and learn to distinguish between. These may include noises in the street, and games that involve guessing which object makes a particular sound.

The document reinforces important messages about child development:

- Children develop at their own rates, and in their own ways.
- The development statements and their order should not be taken as necessary steps for individual children.
- They should not be used as checklists.
- The age/stage bands overlap because these are not fixed age boundaries.

Section review: The wonder that is child development

Thinking

Observation and record keeping can tend to separate areas of development which may lead to a fragmented picture of a child, rather than a view of the whole child. This might also lead to variation in expectations. For example, a tall three year old suggests a physical maturity but the child may display social or language skills which are less advanced. How can we retain a focus on individual development while avoiding making assumptions which might affect expectations for a child?

Reflecting

Review your personal knowledge of typical developmental milestones for:

   i   Birth to two.
   ii Children aged three to five.
   iii Children aged five plus.

Are you comfortable with your knowledge for each age range or is there some CPD you may wish to attend to increase your understanding?

Doing

- Refer to the non-statutory guidance materials *Development Matters in the Early Years Foundation Stage (EYFS)*.
- Select Personal, Social and Emotional Development/Making Relationships. Now track development of a child in your setting under the category: A Unique Child, using all six age bands from birth through to 40–60+ months, to consider development and its progression in this part of Personal, Social and Emotional Development. What questions does this activity raise – is there sufficient information about each area? What other information might you need to use in addition to Development Matters?

The importance of context: nature and nurture

Where a child lives, the experiences he or she has, the family and the local community all have a moulding effect on development in a unique way. Identical twins, for example, brought up in different environments and whose experiences are dissimilar from each other, will not in fact be identical. Their physical appearance is the same, but the context in which they live in those early years powerfully contributes to shaping individual attitudes and beliefs, personality traits, the friends they make and how they communicate with others. Is it nature or nurture that determines children's development? The answer is a mixture of both: nature refers to what we inherit from our parents (genetics) and nurture to the factors in the environment (context) that influence individual development. The interaction of nature and nurture is referred to as the process of epigenesis. Those who support interactionist thinking[6] view the course of development as a 'with' scenario, rather than seeing either nature or nurture as being more influential. Parental legacy and the circumstances and surroundings in which a child grows up work together to influence development, with unique results in every child. A child's genes and the environment he or she grows up in are entangled for the rest of their life.

Psychologist Urie Bronfenbrenner, founder of the Head Start programme in the USA, viewed development as a process that takes place within a set of nested social contexts, with the child at the centre. His bio-ecological model[7] was presented as a set of concentric circles, recognising that all individuals bring their own biological selves to the development process (*bio*), and the social contexts in which development occurs can be thought of as ecosystems, constantly interacting and influencing each other (*ecological*). The research team responsible for the *Early Years Learning and Development Literature Review*[8] which provided the theoretical framework for the revised EYFS, adapted this model and it is a helpful way to understand development as it recognises the enabling contexts that shape individual development.

The research team identified five contextual factors affecting children's development:

Factor	*Implications*
1 Positive relationships	Children's development is influenced by rich, relational experiences that take place both at home and at settings with parents and staff.
2 Children's learning	Imaginative or pretend play, and physical and exploratory play have been identified as important. Narratives through these build language, literacy, cognitive and mathematical development.
3 Rich, appropriate environments	Facilities, specialist equipment and materials are important for children's learning. Guided interaction on the part of the parents and practitioners enhances this learning. The outdoor environment also provides the ideal context to encourage children to cognitively explore and experiment and to move and be active.
4 Partnerships with parents	There are positive links betweenand carers parents' involvement and interest in a child's learning and achievement. Engaging parents in their children's learning can lead to a richer home learning environment which has a positive and enduring impact on children's achievement.
5 Culture	The importance of the cultural context is well-evidenced e.g. social development, in communication and language and in mathematical development.

At the centre of the model is the child. Move outwards to the next layer and this takes in the child's family, regardless of whether this is nuclear, single, extended or multiple. The next layer of influence includes settings outside the immediate family. Here the range is often large, extending to include childminders, play groups, crèches and other childcare providers. The outer layer is the community: friends and neighbours, health services and the local children's centre.

The review put emphasis on the relational factors that influence development, through the many types of interactions that a child experiences in the family, with friends and with practitioners; the physical environment and resources available (these will include play space, physical materials such as sand, water, bricks and mark-making materials) and the routines and particular events in the lives of children (here referring to mealtimes, the daily routine in a setting, celebrations). These in turn are influenced by wider policies and cultural characteristics that serve to inform a child's values and belief systems.

The relationship between the child and the environment operates like a 'serve and return'[9] as in the game of tennis. The adult gives, the child receives; the child gives and the adult receives. Initially, these are the relationships with parents and immediate carers. As a child gets older, others include practitioners, carers and teachers in a widening circle of influence that is in keeping with Bronfenbrenner's ecological model described earlier. How children acquire language is a good example. Take a few minutes to watch interactions between a parent and a baby. You will see the facial expressions, gestures, sounds and babbling of the child being responded to by the parent. The process is mirrored by each partner in this duologue, each playing a role; each responding to the other. What is also important is that such interactions work best when embedded in a caring relationship between the adult and child, as the adult responds to the child's individuality and uniqueness. Such mutual interactions help the acquisition of early language and cement attachment relationships as well as supporting regulation of the emotions. They are also essential to building brain circuitry (i.e. brain cells and their connectives). Genes determine what and when brain circuits are formed (i.e. hard wiring) and instruct the brain on laying down the rules for connecting cells in and across circuits. The experiences a child then has (i.e. soft wiring) shape them. This interplay of genetics and environment is both a continuous and a mutual process.

To stimulate brain development and lay down this kind of properly functioning circuitry, children's early experiences need to be varied and exciting. The brain forms low-level circuits early, and in the initial months, what is needed are sensory, social and emotional experiences. As a child gets older, more sophisticated experiences are needed to shape higher-level circuits. Growing brains thrive on stimulation and active learning (which we return to in a later chapter). The early years are the important years for optimising brain growth. A lack of stimulation inhibits brain growth and can alter the blueprint of a child's life quite dramatically. The brain operates in a 'use it or lose it' manner. A lack of stimulation causes it to prune dendritic growth as neurons compete with each other and only the fittest survive.[10]

As well as being a period of enormous growth, the early years are also a time of vulnerability. Providing proper nutrients, love and stimulating environments to foster learning are crucial. The sponge-like quality of the developing brain makes the circuits vulnerable to the damaging effects of adversity.[11] Stressful experiences, especially during sensitive periods can alter brain circuitry to such an extent that toxic stress in early childhood is now linked to a lifetime of mental and physical illnesses.[12]

Inadequate love and care compromise attachment and future relationships while poor nutrition negatively affects the capacity to learn. A lack of stimulation for the brain lowers the capacity for increased intellectual growth. If a child is constantly carried around and has little encouragement to be physically active, how can we expect the child's physical development to flourish? If there are few opportunities for self-expression how can a child develop emotionally? The course of development may be altered in early childhood by the use of interventions that can change the balance between risk and protection and redress some of the shortfalls in favour of positive outcomes on development and health. While it is possible to plug some of the gaps from a poor foundation, it is a difficult task and less effective than getting it right from the start.[13]

Nature, nurture and the EYFS

There are immediate implications of what brain research tells us on how the EYFS is implemented. As we have described, brain networks change via the learning process and the interactive nature of brain development requires a responsive environment. Resources, first-hand experiences, warm interactions with adults that respond to children's needs and set alight their curiosities are essential. Young brains also need informed practitioners who build upon children's experiences and seek ways to relate to what the child knows and the values they bring to a setting. It requires adults who provide experiences that are interesting and meaningful so that children will enjoy their learning and make connections in what they learn. It requires an approach to learning that enables children to form new ideas confidently, integrate new knowledge and respond to learning actively.

Section review: The importance of context: influencing factors upon development

Thinking

What is your view on the nature versus nature issue? Do you favour one or the other? Do you see it as a balanced combination between the two, or is it an unequal split? What evidence do you have for your decision?

Reflecting

To explore this area further read the Graham Allen Review, *Early Intervention: The Next Steps (2011)*.[14]

Doing

Discuss with colleagues in your setting or school, the five contextual factors that influence development as mentioned in this section. Come to an agreement on how each of these is important for children.

An inclusive framework: supporting life chances for every child

The first thousand days in a child's life are the most important ones and lay the foundations of secure attachment, promote physical growth, build thinking skills and foster early language. The Health Visitor Implementation Plan[15] tells us: *'the period from prenatal development to age three is associated with rapid cognitive language, social, emotional and motor development. A child's early experience and environment influence their brain development during these early years, when warm, positive parenting helps create a strong foundation for the future. New evidence about neurological development and child development highlights just how important prenatal development and the first months and years of life are for every child's future'.*

Brain development in the early years is a significant factor influencing health, learning and behaviour throughout the life cycle. Early experiences and the sort of environments children are exposed to have a significant impact on brain growth, sculpting the architecture of the growing brain. Unlike the rest of the animal kingdom, human brains develop slowly over time – they are flexible and ever changing. The process begins in the womb and continues into adulthood, incorporating what we know as 'sensitive periods', and each of these forms specific circuits which are in turn associated with particular abilities.

Sensitive periods can be thought of as windows of opportunity, short periods of time in development when as humans we are more responsive to influences in the environment. The basic aspects of brain architecture are laid down well before a child enters school.[16] The building process is hierarchical: basic circuits are laid down first and on top of these are laid increasingly more complex circuitry. Circuits build on circuits and skill begets skill.[17]

The brain's capacity for growth enables it to lay down pathways in a sequence that varies little from person to person, and new brain circuits continue to build on circuits that were formed earlier. Such a sequence takes place in all aspects of development, and early experiences build a foundation for lifelong learning, behaviour and health. Strong foundations early in life increase the probability of positive outcomes whereas weak foundations increase the probability of later difficulties.

However, for some children, nature, nurture, or a combination of the two will result in a child with additional needs, which may be physical, intellectual or emotional, or even a combination of these. The EYFS is committed to championing equality for all young children. It is based on the principle that being included is a basic human right for every child. Development Matters[18] confirms this message by saying, *'Children have a right spelled out in the United Nations Convention on the Rights of the Child, to provision which enables them to develop their personalities, talents and abilities irrespective of ethnicity, culture or religion, home language, family background, learning difficulties, disabilities or gender'.*

It is an inclusive framework for every child, which together with a wider set of initiatives aim to better support the life chances of all children. This involves giving parents more control and transferring power to front-line professionals. Sharper accountability is to be placed on schools to make sure that every child fulfils his or her potential, requiring more joined up action between education, health and social care so that GPs, health services, local Sure Start children's centres and other early years services work together in partnership. Getting it right so that all children, including those with particular needs, develop fully and achieve their true potential, however, means sharper legislation and more integrated services to channel resources to those children and families who need it most.

Currently, the life chances of the two million young people in England who have special educational needs fall seriously short of achieving their potential. In comparison with their peers children with disabilities or who have SEN are considerably more likely to be at risk of poor outcomes. They are less likely to achieve well at school and are four times less likely to participate in higher education. In schools, children with SEN are more than twice as likely to be eligible for free school meals than their peers, and pupils at School Action Plus are 20 times more likely to receive a permanent exclusion and seven times more likely to receive a fixed-period exclusion than pupils with no identified special educational need.

In 2011 the Green Paper[19] set out the Government vision to support children with SEN and their families in five clear themes:

- Children's special educational needs are picked up early and support is promptly put in place.
- Staff have knowledge, understanding and skills to support children and young people who have SEN or are disabled.
- Parents know what they can reasonably expect their local school, local college, local authority and local services to provide and are more closely involved in decisions about services.
- Children who would currently have a statement of SEN and young people over 16 who would have a learning difficulty assessment have an integrated

assessment and a single Education, Health and Care Plan which is completed in a shorter time.

- Parents have greater control over the services they and their family use.

Inclusion and the EYFS

In the EYFS, inclusive practice means valuing and respecting diversity, and ensuring that no child or family is discriminated against. Settings which follow inclusive principles promote equality of opportunity where the uniqueness of every child is recognised and valued. It does not mean that all children should be treated the same, but meeting varied needs underlines the importance of understanding child development. The principle of A Unique Child indicates two important messages: firstly that children develop at different rates and secondly that they learn in different ways. With this knowledge, the revised EYFS requires practitioners to consider each child's individual needs, their interests and stage of development and then to use this information to plan challenging and enjoyable experiences in all areas of learning.

In the introduction to the revised EYFS there is the very clear message, '*every child deserves the best possible start in life and the support that enables them to fulfil their potential*'[20] (page 2). Provision for health is high on the Government's agenda and giving every child the best start in life is seen as crucial to reducing health inequalities across the life course. Young children draw on what they know about being healthy from an early age in their play, in their retelling of stories often with puppets, poetry, paintings, dance, music and other modes of the 'hundred languages of children'.[21]

Opportunities for sharing thinking, having conversations with others, playing alone and in pairs or groups promotes confidence and helps children feel good about themselves. Knowledge about health and well-being can be extended through communication and language activities in the home corner, hospital play, with small world and dolls' houses. Discussions at meal times and during food preparation are ideal for quality conversations about keeping healthy.

Reducing health inequalities is not a small task; rather it is an issue of fairness and social justice for everyone in society and addressing these early will continue to be a challenge. Children at risk are often developmentally and academically delayed compared with their more advantaged peers, at least in their early lives. Such gaps open quickly and are difficult to close. The Marmot Review[22] points out that those with higher socio-economic status have a greater array of life chances and more opportunities to lead flourishing lives.

A social gradient in health exists: the lower the social position, the worse for health. One of three priority objectives in the Marmot review was to reduce inequalities in the early development of physical and emotional health, and cognitive, linguistic, and social skills. The review called for greater priority to be given to ensure more expenditure early in the developmental life cycle and for more to be invested in effective interventions.

Children's health and well-being needs are increasingly being met by the range of services offered by Sure Start children's centres, which aim to provide integrated health and family support services to sustain the whole family's needs. The revised EYFS reminds that where a child requires specialist support (page 6), practitioners should link with and help families to access relevant services and other agencies. Many children centres are already providing valuable help and advice with developmental issues. Consultations with the Health Visitors and child development teams provide much needed practical support to parents and a positive boost to early development.

The Government has made a commitment to employ an extra 4,200 health visitors by 2015 in further recognition that health visiting services help children make a positive start in life. The Health Visitor Implementation Plan highlights the special skills of health visitors in supporting early development, for example in delivery of the Healthy Child Programme through Children's Centres, taking a lead on health improvement issues locally, such as advising on healthy eating and emotional well-being; supporting families; and fostering partnerships between health professionals and Children's Centres.

Practitioners are well placed to work with health visitors to intensify support for vulnerable children as part of the Healthy Child Programme health and development review. By 2014, children and young people who would currently have a statement of SEN or learning difficulty assessment will have a single assessment process and an Education, Health and Care Plan to support them from birth to age 25. Clearly, for this to work in practice, close partnership working and systems for information sharing across services are essential.

When a child is between two and three years of age, practitioners must review their progress in a short summary to parents about their child's development in the prime areas. This will be shared with health visitors to allow the professional knowledge of early years practitioners to inform the health visitor-led review at age two. Practitioners decide what the written summary includes but it must highlight areas in which the child is progressing well; areas where extra support may be needed and focus on areas where there are concerns about developmental delay and it must describe the activities and strategies to address issues or concerns.[23] The Early Learning Goals for the end of the reception year can also help to inform decisions on support for vulnerable children.

Healthy development in the early childhood years draws in physical health, social and emotional behaviours and cognitive abilities. The EYFS framework is welcomed for its acknowledgement of health as part of development and the opportunities which can be created for increased joined up action between services to level out the social gradient in health and enable early identification and intervention.

Section review: An inclusive framework: supporting life chances for every child

Thinking

The EYFS is an inclusive framework for every child but to make inclusion work in practice requires better collaboration between professionals in health, education and social services. What successes do you have in this area and what are the potential obstacles to this way of working? What possible solutions might you offer?

Reflecting

Guidance recommends individualised learning to support children's specific needs. Is this provided in your setting? How are children with additional needs supported to access all activities and experiences?

Doing

Read the SEN Green Paper (2011).[24] Consider the implications of this document for practice in your setting or school to meet every child's needs.

Conclusion

This chapter has highlighted the importance of child development in policy and practice. Dame Claire Tickell's words in *The Early Years: Foundations for life, health and learning* set the tone for helping us to think about what laying firm foundations in the early years really means. The chapter made reference to other policy documents (the Allen Review; SEN Green Paper; Marmot Review) which connect development in a wider political and social arena. Understanding how children develop is about much more than knowing what a typical two year old or four year old can do. Of course this is important, but it is only a beginning. Child development should be viewed as change observed over time; change which is observed by informed practitioners with knowledge about all aspects of development. In order to be able to support children's specific and individual needs effectively practitioners should also understand atypical development. Child development is an essential component in the early intervention agenda, aimed at providing a fairer and more inclusive society, which will surely continue to be part of the direction of travel for early years in the future.

Areas of Learning Matter

Aims of the chapter

- To consider a rationale for separating the EYFS areas of learning and development into prime and specific areas
- To assess the influence of 'sensitive periods' in optimal development in the prime areas
- To explore arguments which suggest learning in the specific areas can continue throughout the lifespan
- To consider the changing balance between prime and specific areas over time

As indicated earlier, the six areas of learning in the original EYFS have been extended to seven areas in the revised document. These have then been further separated into two groups to create the prime and specific areas of learning and development shown below:

Prime areas

- Personal, Social and Emotional Development
- Communication and Language
- Physical Development

Specific areas

- Literacy
- Mathematics
- Understanding the World
- Expressive Arts and Design

Rationale for the separation of the areas of learning

This division of the six areas of learning has come about as a result of considerable consultation with the early years sector and with many experts from both within and outside of government, and derives ultimately, from the recommendations made by Dame Clare Tickell, in her review of the EYFS[1] in 2011. We turn our attention now to an explanation of why this division was created.

'Sensitive' periods for development

As indicated in the previous chapter, research shows that there are 'sensitive periods'[2] for certain kinds of development in the early years– when optimal learning can take place. This does not mean that learning cannot take place later; rather it indicates that for some areas of development the earlier it occurs the more efficient it is likely to be. Scientists have shown that the brain changes significantly in relation to learning experiences, describing these changes in terms of the brain's plasticity. This demonstrates how neural connections are established and strengthened for some learning, while others, which are not used, are eliminated in favour of those which are more useful to the individual.

Experience expectant versus experience dependent responses

This adaptability is expressed in the context of two types of brain plasticity: 'experience expectant' and 'experience dependent'. The former *'describes the genetically inclined structural modification of the brain in early life'*, while the latter refers to *'the structural modification of the brain as a result of exposure to complex environments over the lifespan'*.[3] The same distinctions are also proposed in relation to learning, indicating that experience-expectant learning *'takes place when the brain encounters the relevant experience, ideally at an optimal stage,* (or sensitive period), *when a particular biological event is likely to occur best'*.[4] Whereas experience-dependent learning involving: *'mental skills, such as vocabulary acquisition and the ability to see colour do not appear to pass through tight sensitive periods'*[5] so can continue to occur throughout the lifespan.

Early success begets later success debate

Underscoring what has been referred to earlier as the *'early success begets later success'* argument the main reason given for the separation of the curriculum into these two distinct but complementary parts, indicated by Tickell[6] is with reference to a Research Report for The Scottish Council for Research in Education[7] whose aim was to review contemporary research on *'brain function and development and the possible impact on young people's learning'*. In his report, John Hall, the author, focused on the validity and usefulness of the contribution of neuroscience to helping educators understand learning, particularly considering the idea that if some types of learning do not occur early the window of opportunity may be closed for the learner. What Hall delineated was the distinction neuroscientists draw between experience expectant learning and experience dependent learning, stating: *'Experience expectant' learning has been conditioned by our evolutionary development and is where the brain expects certain kinds of input (e.g. visual, tactile or auditory stimulus) to which it will adapt itself. It is a response to our environment which allows the brain to fine-tune itself, and it may be subject to 'sensitive periods' when the brain is particularly ready to respond to these stimuli, which are ever-present in the environment...... The development of speech is 'experience expectant' in that we all have an evolutionary imperative to learn to communicate by speech, and tend to do so at a particular stage of childhood.*[8] Using Hall's analysis, Tickell proposed that because language development, personal, social and emotional development and physical development were significantly different from all other areas they should be admitted to the category of 'experience dependent' learning. This is important for the youngest children because optimal development in these areas occurs earlier rather than later, and although with support children can continue to develop these skills beyond this period, it is evident they do so less efficiently.

Having established these prime areas it was then straightforward for Tickell to identify the remaining areas of learning as specific areas, in terms of cultural or experience dependent learning. Individual to different societies at particular periods in history, or as it relates to cultural norms in a particular place, or with a group, this will be subject to prevailing contemporary views of what is seen as important. Hall's interpretation of this type of learning was: *'Experience dependent' learning does not have these constraints* [of timing in the way that experience expectant learning has]. *It is the type of learning which will only occur if the need arises for it, and tends to be of the sort which features in culturally transmitted knowledge systems. ....learning to read is culturally determined, 'experience dependent', learning, which will not happen by itself, demands training, and results from cultural and social necessity'.*[9] Recognition of the distinction between the two types of learning easily led to a rationale for the separation of the early years curriculum into two distinct groups.

However, in spite of appearing to be cosmetic, overall this division does represent radical change, in as much as, what were previously considered to be inseparable areas of learning are now set out as distinct groups, suggesting that initially the prime areas are of greater importance than the specific areas, a discussion to which we will return in other chapters.

Areas of development and learning

Exploring further this re-configuration of the areas of learning in the EYFS (2012), we see the focus of the prime areas being on the developing child, while the focus in the specific areas is on the knowledge, skills and understanding associated with learning domains in a school-type curriculum. A comparison between the original EYFS (2007) and revised EYFS (2012) areas of learning is shown below: (see Figure 1).

Area of Learning (brackets, indicate original EYFS area)	Aspects (original) 2007	Aspects (revised) 2012	
Communication and Language (previously Communication, Language and Literacy)	1. Language for Communication 2. Language for Thinking	1. Listening and Attention 2. Understanding 3. Talking	
Physical Development	1. Movement and Space 2. Health and Bodily Awareness 3 Using Equipment and Materials	1. Moving and Handling 2. Health and Self-Care	**Prime areas** (focusing on child development)
Personal, Social and Emotional Development	1. Dispositions and Attitudes 2. Self-confidence and Self-esteem 3. Making Relationships 4. Behaviour and Self-control 5. Self-care 6. Sense of Community	1. Self-confidence and self-awareness 2. Managing feelings and behaviour 3. Making relationships	
Literacy (previously Communication, Language and Literacy)	1. Linking Sounds and Letters 2. Reading 3. Writing 4. Handwriting	1. Reading 2. Writing	**Specific areas** (focusing on application of curriculum 'subjects')
Mathematics (previously Problem Solving, Reasoning and Numeracy)	1. Numbers as Labels and for Counting 2. Calculating 3. Shape, Space and Measures	1. Numbers 2. Shape, Space and Measures	

Understanding the World (previously Knowledge and Understanding of the World)	1. Exploration and Investigation 2. Designing and Making 3. ICT 4. Time 5. Place 6. Communities	1. People and Communities 2. The World 3. Technology	**Specific areas** (focusing on application of curriculum 'subjects')
Expressive Arts and Design (previously Creative Development)	1. Being Creative Responding to Experiences, Expressing and Communicating Ideas 2. Exploring Media and Materials 3. Creating Music and Dance 4. Developing Imagination and Imaginative Play	1. Exploring and using media and materials 2. Being Imaginative	

Figure 1

Balance between prime and specific areas

The EYFS (2012)[10] indicates: *'Practitioners working with the youngest children are expected to focus strongly on the three prime areas, which are the basis for successful learning in the other four (specific) areas. The three prime areas reflect the key skills and capacities all children need to develop and learn effectively, and become ready for school'*. The espoused aim of this approach is to ensure that young children are ready to benefit from their experiences when they start school at the end of the EYFS – so we might conclude that there should be a focus on only developing children's skills in the prime areas. However this is complicated by the statement that: *'All practitioners must consider the individual needs, interests, and stage of development of each child in their care, and must use this information to plan a challenging and enjoyable experience for each child in all of the areas of learning and development.'*[11] So what conclusions can we reach about judging the timeliness of the introduction of the prime versus the specific areas?

Since it is obvious that the prime areas are considered highly significant for young children's learning it seems to be clear that there is a will to get the basics right for the youngest children. This is because, as has been indicated earlier, many children, particularly the most disadvantaged, struggle to benefit fully from their early education entitlement because of speech, communication and conduct/behavioural difficulties. It is also recognised that when children struggle in these areas their chances of succeeding later are significantly reduced. Therefore we must assume that the purpose behind this balance is to help to establish the prime areas fully so that children can indeed benefit from the experiences on offer to them. Returning to the EYFS (2012) the document states: '*It is expected that the balance will shift towards a more equal focus on all areas of learning as children grow in confidence and ability within the three prime areas*'.[12] This suggests that those children in pre-school, nursery or reception classes with good speech, communication, personal, social and emotional and physical development would experience a growing emphasis on the specific areas, while those who needed more support in the prime areas would receive it, with planned support in any areas as necessary. Getting the balance right will be a professional judgement relying on practitioners' expertise and knowledge of child development which we have discussed in the previous chapter.

Section review: Prime and specific areas of learning

Thinking

Reference has been made in this chapter to the fact that speech development may be subject to sensitive periods while vocabulary acquisition can continue to occur throughout the lifespan. Why is this important and how has this difference been explained in terms of brain development?

Reflecting

Does the rationale for separating the areas of learning in the way described make sense to you? Why? Why not?

Doing

How will the new emphasis between the prime and specific areas of the EYFS impact on your practice? Consider the ages and stages of children in your group. This is likely to be significantly different if you are working with the very youngest or oldest children. List some of the major implications for your work. In the following chapters we will consider the role of the prime and specific areas.

Prime Areas of Learning Matter

Aims of the chapter

- To explore a rationale for the prime areas of learning in the revised EYFS (2012)
- To identify the significance of Communication and Language to children's development and learning
- To explore the role of Personal, Social and Emotional Development and the importance of attachment relationships to the development of a sense of self and self-confidence in young children
- To consider the lasting impact of early attitudes to Physical Development and healthy eating

Rationale for the prime areas of learning in the revised EYFS (2012)

The importance of the prime areas of learning for young children's development cannot be overstated as they contribute to all aspects of personal development. For example, a significant aspect of learning in infancy is in relation to the young baby's sense of being a person. Early interaction acts as a model or representation of relationships and the young baby adapts and responds to these and lives in the expectation that future relationships will be like these (there is further reference to this throughout this book). Therefore early interactions and relationships are not only important in terms of communication and language itself but are also fundamental to a child's sense of self, self-worth and self-efficacy, supporting their health and well-being, if they are cared for and responded to with kindness, warmth and approval.

When we study young babies we cannot fail also to observe that communication is literally embodied, in that babies communicate not only through gestures and sounds but also physically, using their bodies in what is often described as a 'dance' of communication and interaction. These dynamic strands of development are interdependent since they do not occur in isolation but in concert: communication contributing to the baby's sense of self as well as his or her ability to communicate; physical development driving cognition and playing its part in communication, and language development deriving from interaction and relationships. This is well illustrated in written guidance for practitioners working with babies and toddlers where it is stated: *'a young baby's cry may simultaneously represent the beginning of communication (language development), a tool for getting needs met (intellectual development), and a way of relating to others (social emotional development).*[1] These discrete but connected areas all contribute to healthy development both in real life and in the EYFS because they are important for children's health and well-being and are the foundations of all future learning (See Figure 1)

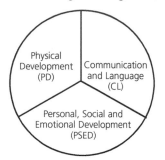

Figure 1 The prime areas of learning

It seems wise to assume therefore that when we are thinking about, or working with the very youngest children, the three prime areas should be considered together. However this does not preclude considering children's development in each area separately, which we will now do. We will begin with why Communication and Language is considered to be so important to children's learning, health and well-being before examining what is involved in effective communication and language for young children in the EYFS.

Why Communication and Language is important

Neuroscience tells us: '*The brain is biologically primed to acquire language right from the very start of life; the process of language acquisition needs the catalyst of experience. There is an inverse relationship between age and the effectiveness of learning many aspects of language – in general, the younger the age of exposure, the more successful the learning*'.[2] It is obvious from these findings that the development of good communication and language is essential if young children are to acquire the skills they need to become effective communicators. This is further emphasised by research which proposes that communication and language skills are '*fundamental building blocks for a child's development*', suggesting that '*Language difficulties can impact on emotional development with resultant behavioural difficulties and problems forming friendships*'.[3] If evidence of the need for a greater emphasis on communication and language development in the early years is required we need look no further than these words and those of the popular press whose headlines characterise children's speech problems as resulting from: '*Prolonged Use of Pacifier Linked to Speech Problems*'[4] and forward-facing buggies. Recent findings cited by ICAN,[5] the children's communication charity, showed that upwards of 50% of children at school entry point are starting out with poor language skills, find it hard to listen and because of speech, language and communication needs are already at a disadvantage by the time they begin school.

The basis of listening and attention begins even before birth when mothers communicate with the unborn child through talking to them and listening to music with the baby. Intertwined with the development of communication and language are the relationships that start while the baby is in the womb – through mother and family members relating to the unborn baby either directly, by talking to them and touching the mother's stomach, or indirectly when they refer to the baby in discussions. A recent review of the evidence showed that the relationship between the mother and baby is highly significant for early language development in young children[6] since language is as much an outcome of warm relationships in which joint attention and inter-subjectivity lead to shared meanings and new understandings, as mother/adult and baby interact, as it as a biological drive. Indeed it could be argued the two are symbiotic.

While personal characteristics such as being able to hear well and being able to remember and use language are important in terms of the ability to develop and use speech, the social dimensions of language have also been revealed to be highly significant since they shape the child's communicative competence. Studies have also shown that different types of communicative environments make a difference to children's outcomes since some (often more advantaged homes) are calculated to offer many more words per hour than others (where quantity of words heard is indicative of expanded discussions, many of which are positive and affirmative). In homes where there is less talk (often more disadvantaged economically and socially) the nature of interaction tends to be business-like, contains fewer affirmations and is connected with the here and now.[7] The development of a wide vocabulary is associated with the quantity of talk heard and this in turn influences children's ability to socialise with others and their readiness to learn to read when more formal school learning commences. The effect of this is that children from homes where there is less talk are put at a disadvantage in terms of their language development. Compounding this problem, for the most disadvantaged children, it has been shown that exposure to story/book reading at age three, which has an impact on the child's ability to develop 'book talk' and vocabulary while at the same time widening the child's general knowledge, occurs less frequently, relative to the lower socio-economic status of families involved.[8]

Communication and Language in the EYFS

Communication and Language is set out under three aspects in the revised EYFS:

1 Listening and Attention
2 Understanding
3 Speaking

Listening and Attention

The first of these is concerned with the child's ability to attend to sounds, beginning with responding to their own name and familiar voices, leading ultimately to them being able to listen attentively while their attention may be focused on something else at the same time. For example, they might follow instructions about how to plant a seed while listening to a discussion about the necessary conditions for the seed to grow properly.

Understanding

'Understanding' is the term used to describe children's receptive language; defined as the *'mental store of words and phrases'*[9] this highlights the child's knowledge of what is being communicated and what he/she understands but is not yet able to say. An example of this is the 15 month old toddler who can run to fetch a ball from across the room when asked by a familiar person to do so, but who would be unable to say 'I am fetching the ball'. This is an important area in terms of young children with EAL, many of whom have good understanding of what is being said but who are not yet ready to use talk in the same way as their peers, for whom English is a first language. This aspect of communication is particularly significant for children listening to a story that is told, rather than shared through a book, and for being able to follow sequences in instructions such as 'first, then, before, next' and so on.

Speaking

Speaking, or expressive language, is the aspect of language that is more easily observed and because of this it appears simpler to make judgments about children's competence in this area. However it is more complex than first appears because it is multi-dimensional and contains within it the *'ability to create and communicate meaning which involves representing, speaking and writing.*[10] It also includes language production such as making sounds, articulating strings of sounds and learning word meanings and grammatical constructions.

Indeed, learning to speak a language involves many dimensions including:

- phonology: getting to grips with the sound patterns of language and being able to divide words into syllables
- morphology: understanding the meaning and structure of words
- syntax: the grammar or structure of sentences
- semantics: interpreting the meaning of what is conveyed in spoken language.[11]

When we consider language in this way it highlights that what we often take for granted is actually a very sophisticated process. While almost all children will learn a language, communicating effectively is a major shift, which relies on having the capability to communicate, alongside being exposed to good role models and this starts with the first attachment relationship.

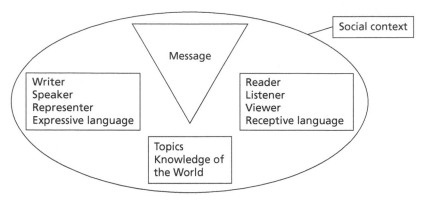

Figure 2 The communication triangle based on Walmsley

In order for children to be able to communicate and use language effectively they need people to communicate with and they need to have experiences which ignite their interests and motivate them to talk about their experiences. This has been summed up in the *'communication triangle'* based on Aristotelian theory devised by Walmsley[12] in which it is shown that the relationships through which writers, speakers and listeners create and express ideas is positioned within a social context that both influences and controls the nature of interactions because of the receivers, that is, the readers, listeners and viewers, together with the theories, topics or ideas which are under discussion.[13]

Section review: Why Communication and Language is important

Thinking

Communication is often described as a 'two-way street'. From your reading of this section, explore the significance of two important aspects of language: receptive and expressive language, described in the EYFS as Listening and Attention and Understanding.

Reflecting

Since the communication triangle comprises conveyers and receivers of information as well as topics for discussion, what is the role of the practitioner beyond encouraging children's communication and language through interacting with them?

Doing

Using the notion of the communication triangle referred to in this section identify how communication and language works in your setting. You may be able to take notes or ask a colleague to observe interaction in the setting. Try to select two or three representative periods of about 45 minutes to an hour in any day to identify the focus of adult-child interactions. These will vary and will range from discussions, such as:

- the here and now (the weather, for example)
- practical issues such as whether a child has brought a coat or put their dinner money or comforter in the correct place
- behaviour and rules, including hygiene practices
- comforting distressed or upset children
- talking about learning, for example: discussing a story, comparing which of two children is taller, whose turn it is to feed the guinea pig and so on.

Analyse the proportion of talk related to each of the above and any other areas that emerge from your observations.
Review what this tells you about:

- the purpose and nature of talk in your setting
- the quality of talk
- the speakers
- the listeners
- the topics.

Evaluate
- The balance between adult talk and child talk
- The range of topics discussed and what provoked richer, more meaningful discussions.
- Discuss with colleagues the implications of your findings.

The next area we will consider is Personal, Social and Emotional Development which is the context for communication and language.

Why Personal, Social and Emotional Development is important

Personal, Social and Emotional Development has been described as the 'bedrock' for children's development. It contributes to all other aspects of their development because it shapes beliefs about who they are, what they can do and what other people are like. It is accepted that Personal, Social and Emotional Development skills should be established right from the start because, although *'windows of opportunity' …for skill development and behavioural adaptation remain open for many years, trying to change behaviour or build new skills on a foundation of brain circuits that were not wired properly when they were first formed is much harder and requires more intensive effort'.*[14] This is summed up in an independent report to the government in which it is argued: *'There is abundant evidence …….. to suggest that the first three years of life create the foundation in learning how to express emotion and to understand and respond to the emotions of others. Lessons learnt in this period can last a lifetime, and prepare an individual to progress physically, mentally and emotionally at every stage of life …... That is not to say that we do not develop socially and emotionally after this stage. However, lessons not learnt in this formative period become harder and harder to learn later in life, and the longer the delay the more it sets up the individual to fail in later life'.*[15]

Influences on cognition

It is also a well-established fact that emotion and cognition are closely linked: if a child's emotional needs are met they are much more able to benefit from their experiences and to learn.[16] The significant responsibility of adults in day-care and school settings is obvious here too because it is *'in the context of relationships that infants and toddlers … develop expectations about how the world is, how the adults in the world behave, and their own place in the social world'.*[17]

A further reason why Personal, Social and Emotional Development is important is that young children who exhibit healthy social, emotional, and behavioural adjustment are more likely to have good academic performance in primary school.[18] The case for supporting children to develop as rounded individuals in the early years is strong – since this is the period when children learn most rapidly and form opinions about themselves and others. Given the number of hours young children spend in day-care and/or in schools during the EYFS stage it is important to be aware of the influence this formative period can have on young children's psychological well-being, their beliefs, their self-belief and their attitudes to other people.

Personal, Social and Emotional Development in the EYFS

Personal, Social and Emotional Development is set out under three aspects in the revised EYFS:

1 Self-confidence and Self-awareness
2 Managing Feelings and Behaviour
3 Making Relationships

Self-confidence and Self-awareness

If Personal, Social and Emotional Development is the bedrock upon which young children's development is built it could be argued that self-confidence and self-awareness are its cornerstones since this aspect of Personal, Social and Emotional Development helps the child to define themselves as a person, recognising their own preference for some things over others, enabling them to decide whether they need support from others, or not; as well as driving their confidence to try new things and to talk about their ideas. These, and other skills in this area of learning, have been described as 'soft skills' which can be defined as: *'personal attributes that enhance an individual's interactions ..... soft skills are interpersonal and broadly applicable. Soft skills are often described by using terms often associated with personality traits, such as:*

- *optimism*
- *common sense*
- *responsibility*
- *a sense of humor*
- *integrity'.*[19]

This is noteworthy in as much as it could be argued that these skills are not usually used with reference to children's development in the early years. Yet after a further examination it is evident that all but the trait of integrity (which is never in question where young children are concerned) are often seen in young children. Indeed most three year olds display optimism daily as they awaken to the possibilities of a new day ahead; common sense when presented with problems such as deciding what materials to use to make a bird table; responsibility for putting their shoes away (provided they have previously been supported to do this) and a sense of humour when they recognise a simple joke or laugh at a funny ending to a story. The outcomes for this area are:

> 'children are confident to try new activities, and say why they like some activities more than others. They are confident to speak in a familiar group, will talk about their ideas, and will choose the resources they need for their chosen activities. They say when they do or don't need help.'[20]

Managing Feelings and Behaviour

The second aspect of Personal, Social and Emotional Development Managing Feelings and Behaviour was arguably present in the earlier EYFS document (2007) but its importance is now further emphasised since it is has become one of just three, rather than six aspects, as previously. The outcomes expressed in the Early Learning Goal for this aspect are that:

> 'Children talk about how they and others show feelings, talk about their own and others' behaviour, and its consequences, and know that some behaviour is unacceptable. They work as part of a group or class, and understand and follow the rules. They adjust their behaviour to different situations, and take changes of routine in their stride'.[21]

Essentially this is a departure from the stiff upper lip policy of the past as policy makers, researchers and educators alike have recognised that feelings and behaviour are intimately connected. While one can ignore feelings at a conscious level, unconsciously feelings that are not addressed are often suppressed to emerge later in tantrums, displays of challenging behaviour, aggression and depression, none of which are helpful long term to the health of young children nor to those around them as they grow into adults unable to handle their own feelings or those of others.

Several studies have shown the value of focusing on this area to improve children's life skills and life chances. For example, when children were taught to understand their own emotions and other people's, to handle conflicts and to problem-solve and to relate to others emotionally it was found that problem behaviours reduced and social skills increased.[22] The WAVE Trust whose aim is to end abuse of all children indicated in a seminal report, that '*To the best of current knowledge, the sensitivity window for emotional sensitivity and empathy lies within the first 18 months of life, and these 'skills' are shaped by the prime carer's interaction style. The wrong style can have disastrous results'.*[23] This finding accentuates the importance of the role of parents, and the key person (for those young children who spend long periods of time in day-care), since the association between emotional attachment, warmth and attunement are highly significant for outcomes in managing feelings and behaviour. When young children are in day-care they rely on carers to provide them with the right style of interaction which is respectful and which meets their needs and it is important in providing this care (in place of parents) that practitioners working with children of all ages remember that '*For a child away from home 'the lack of a sense of time means that separation feels like an eternity'.*[24]

Recognising and acting on this knowledge (about the child's feelings) to create the conditions that make separation from the primary caregiver manageable for the baby or young child demonstrates empathy with the child: '*Empathy begins with the realisation of a sense of oneness with the other. In this feeling of identification with the other or 'affect Attunement', the sense of oneness is accompanied by a positive evaluation of the other. These nourishing emotions develop only in a context of warm, loving infant-caregiver interaction, and not in conditions of ...... hostility or rejection'.*[25] It is therefore essential that practitioners not only 'care' for children's emotions but when working with parents of very young children they offer support that helps parents

'tune-in' to their children in ways that will support their emotional development, particularly their ability to manage and regulate their feelings. The regulation and appraisal of the emotions is fundamental to self-organisation and '*self-regulation is at the core of the self'.*[26] It is therefore essential that practitioners caring for

children focus on helping them to identify, name, own and work through their feelings in ways that are supportive to the child. This practice should lead to young children being able to understand and manage their own feelings, while encouraging them to recognise that everybody experiences a range of feelings some of which can at times be very unpleasant and uncomfortable. These discussions can lead into helping children to find positive ways of responding to their own and others' feelings.

Making Relationships

The final aspect of Personal, Social and Emotional Development Making Relationships is both an outcome and a necessary ingredient of the two other aspects of this area of development. Making relationships is about how children are helped to interact with one another positively, undertaking shared experiences, cooperating with others and being sensitive to others' needs and feelings. The expectations for children's outcomes in this aspect would be demanding for many adults since they require a good deal of 'self and other awareness' which is heavily dependent on children having had consistent role models on which to base their ideas of appropriate behaviour. A substantial number of children do have high empathy from experiencing relatively secure attachments, however a significant percentage of children are believed to suffer insecure, avoidant and ambivalent attachments and as a result may exhibit many behaviours of concern including conduct behaviour disorders, as well as/and/or becoming bullies or victims of bullying. The latter has been identified as '*a common problem with potentially long-lasting consequences for victims*'.[27] According to an Ofsted[28] survey, 39% of children reported being bullied in the 12 months prior to its 2008 report, although estimates of prevalence varied widely between studies, mainly because of differences in definition'.[29] In order to counteract or reduce incidences of bullying it is vital that young children learn to feel good about themselves through experiences and interactions which help them to develop a positive sense of themselves across the multiple realities of who they are and what they are like, related to:

- Appearance: including skin tone, hair type, hair colour and ethnicity.
- Personality: including the things a child likes/dislikes chooses/does not choose to do.
- Family: including who is in their family, the people they like to be with/ are important to them.

- Culture: including their family composition, their traditions, beliefs and practices.
- Capabilities: what they can do alone/with help.

Through being helped to know and understand what they are like (their identity) children can be supported to appreciate and value their similarities (with other children and/or family members) and the differences between themselves and others.

Self-acceptance can lead to acceptance of others as accepting ourselves is one of the defining dimensions of what it is to be human and helping children to success-fully negotiate this journey is a challenge for parents and educators alike. The benefits to children are significant since several studies have shown that emotionally well-adjusted children have better chances of success in their school outcomes and are able to build positive relationships and have a much greater chance of academic success[30] – a factor which also improves people's overall sense of well-being. The outcomes for this aspect of Personal Social and Emotional Development are:

> 'children play co-operatively, taking turns with others. They take account of one another's ideas about how to organise their activity. They show sensitivity to others' needs and feelings, and form positive relationships with adults and other children'.[31]

Section review: Why Personal, Social and Emotional Development is important

Thinking

Having read this section, consider which aspects of Personal, social and emotional development are most closely connected to Communication and Language, discussed in the previous section.

Reflecting

How are less confident children in your setting, who may have experienced less rewarding relationships with adult carers, supported to express and manage their feelings?

> **Doing**
> Identify some children in your group who are more confident than others.
>
> List:
> a) how they demonstrate this self-confidence
> b) how adults and other children respond to them.
>
> Identify the less confident children in your group.
>
> List:
> a) how adults and children respond to them
> b) how these children are supported to make relationships with other children.
>
> Identify ways that you, staff and confident children in your setting could improve the confidence of less confident children to help them develop relationships with other children more easily.

We will now consider Physical Development which is important not only in its own right but also because of its influence on other aspects of development including PSED.

Why Physical Development is important

Physical development is fundamental to all other development, beginning in the womb, in the first trimester, with the fish-like movements of the foetus, which involve frequent motion, in response to sounds, or to avoid an oncoming object such as a needle, continuing as the baby develops to the point when it is ready to swim down the birth canal. Because of the immaturity of the human neonate it is argued that the first nine months following birth are *'in effect the second half of gestation'*.[32] Physical development has also been categorised as 'experience-expectant' learning which means that the brain is wired in expectation of this development. Physical development also supports the maintenance of a healthy weight and the development of strong bones, muscles and heart as well as the development of personal and social skills. Indeed many would argue that every aspect of human development is intrinsically connected to this area.

After birth babies' movements are strongly connected to their social and emotional development, for example, turning towards a familiar voice or making eye contact by gazing at people's faces. At the same time as connecting them with people, movement allows them to explore their surroundings through grasping and holding objects and reaching out to touch things.

As they gain control of the upper body they are able to bring objects to the mouth where further sensory exploration begins. Through movement of the lower body they are able to explore the environment by kicking, pushing, creeping, crawling, pulling to stand and eventually walking. These movements involve development of the muscles, bones and joints as well as the vestibular system, which is responsible for balance and helps the baby or young child know where they are in space. Indeed the development of this system is reliant on movement and it occurs naturally as an outcome of young children's routine play such as rocking on a horse, riding on a swing or climbing and jumping.

Physical development is not only essential for developing the systems that allows the child to gain control of the body it also has a significant influence on learning. Indeed the vestibular system supplies 'our brains with a sense of direction, and [supports] many higher cognitive skills such as reading and writing [which] require directional awareness'.[33] Competence in writing relies heavily on the early skills babies develop as they succeed in strengthening their shoulders and arms and in their ability to coordinate movements to achieve the pincer grasp: 'grasping an object between the thumb and forefinger.'[34]

Crawling is another developmental milestone important in itself but also for its contribution in reinforcing the child's ability to cross the body's midline, thus developing directionality, a skill which becomes important in writing from left to right.[35] Sadly, it has been shown that babies who have been severely neglected do not develop normally. Indeed, in one study where children were 'cared for' (fed, kept clean and clothed) but under stimulated, isolated and deprived of affection the majority were unable to walk or talk by three years of age,[36] indicating that while the potential to develop these skills was present the motivation, opportunity, encouragement and drive to do so was not.

Physical Development in the EYFS

Physical Development in the EYFS is set out under two aspects in the revised EYFS:

1 Moving and Handling
2 Health and Self-Care

Moving and Handling

Moving and Handling relates to movement and coordination of the body. This is fundamental to child development since it addresses the ways in which children develop control of their bodies through physical activity. While most people would agree that young children need frequent physical activity since it is the fulcrum of their development this area is often given less status than it deserves. This view of physical development may have contributed to increases in children's sedentary behaviour.

Vigorous play has certainly reduced in recent years, to the extent that a recent Department of Health report[37] recommended that children aged five and under who are capable of walking unaided should increase their physical activity by at least 30 minutes a day to at least 180 minutes – taken over the course of a day rather than in long bursts. Explained in part by parental anxieties for their children of stranger danger and to an increase in play with technological devices, this reduction in physical activity is worrying. Another reason why physical play and activity may have reduced is because of misunderstandings about its role in children's development and a lack of awareness of its considerable benefits physically and emotionally to children. This is a particular concern because it is now widely accepted that it is in the early years that children are establishing patterns of activity which will affect their future lives. If the importance of activity (and healthy eating) begin early in a child's life these good habits tend to become fixed. So starting early is paramount if less desirable habits are not to become the norm for some children. Given the massive impact physical development has on children's sense of self-confidence and self-efficacy and on their learning this area should not be overlooked or taken for granted.

While physical development appears to simply unfold it doesn't just happen and is dependent on a range of factors, among which are prenatal factors (for example a mother's exposure to cigarette smoke, chemicals or other agents), inherent characteristics, nutrition and an environment that encourages and motivates the child to find out what he or she can do within safe limits.

Physical skills can be categorised in many ways and the main areas for gross motor development involve coordination, balance and spatial awareness however we address these through considering the following groups:

- locomotor skills: running, jumping, hopping, galloping, skipping, dancing
- stability skills: balance, riding a bike, climbing, 'freezing', taking weight and moving using different parts of the body (back, tummy)
- object-control skills: kicking, catching, throwing, striking, and rolling a ball.

Locomotor skills

Much emphasis is often placed on the first of the above: locomotor skills. These can be developed through everyday activities provided children are given the time and space to engage in them. If we observe the gait of the two or three year old running we notice movement is less than fluid as young children learn to coordinate the lower limbs and the upper body to move forward while maintaining a firm grip on the ground to control their movements. However, as children grow to young adulthood these differences become less and less obvious and if we observe expert performance we notice tight muscle tone, flexibility, speed and many other signs which indicate a trained performance. These show that a person has honed their control beyond the everyday skills that most reasonably fit adults demonstrate. We don't need to support children to become expert runners, jumpers or dancers in the early years but what we do need to do is understand the complexity involved in body movement and encourage and motivate children to enjoy and partake in locomotor activities so that they continue to benefit from them well beyond the door of the reception class.

Stability skills

Stability skills are not always given sufficient emphasis in the early years since these often involve the psychological, if not the physical support of an adult. Balancing is something we often notice in its absence: the child in the reception class who is unable to stand on one foot comes to our attention, as does the child who seems uncoordinated – spilling her drink, slipping off a chair or not being able to fix or fasten things. These activities all require stability skills and can be underdeveloped when children are restricted in their movements. Indeed sitting or standing requires balance and involves quite a lot of effort by the young child which is why it is considered inappropriate to have young children seated for more than a short period at any one time.

Object control

Object control skills are often considered to be caught, rather than taught. The skills of catching and throwing are not as simple as they often seem. This is because in order to throw effectively, the child has to make judgements about the action of a ball: different balls or other objects will behave differently due to varying weights and composition, so a dense heavy ball will be more difficult to throw and catch for a younger child than a larger lighter ball. This is because of the fine and large motor skills required to handle, grip and project the ball at the same time as accurately judging the distance from the thrower to the target and assessing the amount of thrust to project the ball accurately. Conversely, catching the ball combines a number of skills, including positioning the lower body and limbs with weight spread to maintain balance, while visually tracking the trajectory of the ball and positioning the arms and hands ready to reach out accurately when the ball finally falls through the air. Children need help to develop these skills and plenty of uninterrupted time to practise and perfect them.

Hand-eye coordination

Among many other skills the latter all require hand-eye control which is one of the biggest early challenges the young child has to achieve, involving development of the muscles in the wrist, hand and fingers, at the same time as developing the visual acuity to focus on an object while reaching towards it and generating the larger muscle movements of shoulder and arm. Effortless though these movements appear they take considerable skill to perfect and they continue to develop and become more refined as children mature. The journey from immature reaching and grasping by the baby to the fine, controlled movements of the toddler mark-making with a crayon, to those of the young child handling a pencil with good control is vast. The skills involved in using writing tools are also worthy of further mention here since these have rightly been placed in the outcomes for Physical Development in the EYFS (2012) rather than in Writing, as previously.

Pencil control

Much emphasis is placed on the skills of manipulating and handling tools in schools and early years settings, particularly the skills connected with writing tools. These are both necessary and useful since children will still use the written word as a form of communication for some time to come. Leaving aside children's understanding of the representational side of writing, the physical demands of making marks on paper are quite an achievement when they finally emerge. They include holding a writing tool in a way that will allow them to make a specific, rather than a random mark. This requires the ability to grasp the pen or pencil tightly while applying sufficient pressure not to tear through the paper or break the pencil point but enough to make marks on the paper in the selected place. Younger children can become quite proficient at making marks randomly using a range of writing tools but find thicker felt pens much easier to manipulate than pens or pencils which require significant pressure to make a mark.

Learning how to use a writing tool efficiently doesn't mean that children have to practise these skills endlessly since many of the same fine motor skills are developed by activities such as: threading objects; joining in with action rhymes; fixing items together – such as Lego, Mobilo and construction materials; pressing, turning and pulling knobs, levers or pages; finger painting and interacting with technology on a keyboard, iPad or Smartphone. The challenge for practitioners is to ensure that they observe children to identify each child's development in this area so that they can then plan opportunities for children to practise and refine certain skills in activities and experiences that are intensely motivating and developmentally appropriate for individual children. Children who have the physical capacity to hold and manipulate writing tools will, in time and with support from more skilled others, seek out ways of communicating and representing their thoughts through mark-making, drawing and writing, areas we will return to in following chapters. The outcomes for Moving and Handling are:

> 'children show good control and co-ordination in large and small movements. They move confidently in a range of ways, safely negotiating space. They handle equipment and tools effectively, including pencils for writing.'[38]

Health and Self-Care

The outcomes for this aspect of Physical Development are:

> 'children know the importance for good health of physical exercise, and a healthy diet, and talk about ways to keep healthy and safe. They manage their own basic hygiene and personal needs successfully, including dressing and going to the toilet independently'.[39]

Many schools and settings already help children to achieve these outcomes very successfully in what is a challenging domain. However a more incremental approach to teaching these skills could ensure that by the time children reached the end of the EYFS they would be better prepared for some of the challenges they face in Key Stage 1, and beyond the school gates, to make more healthy choices. So for example children of three or four years old are good at the rhetoric of knowing which foods and activities are healthy but given a choice choose the ones they like rather than the ones they 'know' would be good for them. That is often a function of their immaturity but it may also be because they receive mixed or confused messages about food and exercises from many sources – including television, home, school or setting and adult role models.

Healthy eating

Food is a difficult area for many people – not just children. Babies and young children prefer sweetness before any other taste, so helping children to try a range of tastes is something that is well worth spending time on so that they develop preferences for different foods, rather than being limited to only a small range. One of the most important influences apart from their wellness and food tolerance is the modeling they observe, conveying to them that other adults and children enjoy eating this particular food, or trying this new drink. It is salutary too to remember that whatever culture children are born into they learn to share the food that is eaten by their family and community so, many of the fads and dislikes children develop towards certain foods may well be indicative of what they deduce from implicit, rather than explicit messages, telling them that some foods are 'not for them'.

Physical exercise

A similar situation can happen in respect of keeping healthy through physical exercise and while parents and other adults might verbally encourage children to be active they often confuse children by *doing* something different from what they *say* – for example, taking children to the setting or school by car instead of walking. Children are true reflectors of the messages they receive even though sometimes adult don't mean to convey them! Exercise is just one area where children will 'read between the lines' to work out adults' true beliefs about the importance of physical activity.

Self-help skills

Self-help skills become a matter of pride with young children who are praised and rewarded regularly for their efforts in taking off or putting on articles of clothing or shoes, pumps, or wellingtons, or who go to the toilet initially with support and subsequently unaided. The conditions that promote this sense of pride are brought about by adults who really understand children's development, who know that independence is an outcome of having been allowed to be dependent for as long as is necessary and who recognize that independently visiting the bathroom area can be very daunting for young children – especially if they have just moved from one room to another or from one setting to another. So it is important for settings to take account of this, especially at times of transition. Other areas for consideration in relation to this aspect are:

Helping children to try a variety of food and to understand why we eat certain foods:

- **The food pyramid:** Use displays to show the range of foods to be eaten and to identify what the food does to help growth and development.
- **Grow edible plants** such as strawberries, tomatoes, lettuce and potatoes and prepare and eat them in the setting or school.

Helping children to care for themselves:

- Encourage children to **care for their teeth** by talking about the things that are good for oral health and the things that they should try to do to encourage their teeth to remain healthy.
- **Use puppets to model** aspects of health and self-care.

Helping children to understand about hygiene and infection control:

- **Runny noses and colds:** Provide tissues at an accessible level close to an enclosed bin – display reminders about hygiene for nose-blowing and coughing.

Helping children to make healthy choices:

- Encourage children to **feel proud of achievements** in health and self-care.

Section review: Why Physical Development is important

Thinking

Physical development focuses on a number of personal issues which may present challenges for practice. From your reading of the previous section, identify which aspects of healthy eating you already promote. Are you confident that parents and practitioners have a common view of what constitutes healthy eating? If not, what could you do to promote this?

Reflecting

When you plan for physical activity do you consider each child's locomotor, stability and object-control skills? Why? Why not?

Doing

Audit the bathroom area for two to five year olds to consider how to make it a child-friendly area so that children don't get worried about using it:
Location: Distance from the main indoor and outdoor areas.
Noise levels: Is it a very quiet area (too quiet?); A very noisy area (not quiet enough?); A moderately noisy area (just right?); How do you know – did you ask the children, have parents asked their children and told you?
Appearance: Is the area bright, well-lit and pleasantly appointed?
Facilities: Are the doors easy to open? Are toilet roll/sinks/water/soap and towels or driers easily accessible?
Signage: Is there a visual reminder of the five sequence hand wash?

Conclusion

The prime areas represent those aspects of children's development which are most malleable and vulnerable at the same time. As we have discussed previously, nature and nurture both have their part to play in young children's physical, personal, social, emotional and communicative development. However it has been proved that although development appears to unfold 'naturally', in truth optimum healthy development emerges under auspicious conditions in which attentive, concerned, warm, caring adults provide the raw materials from which the child is able to build the self.

The term 'secure base', coined by Ainsworth in her research into children's differing styles of attachments to their parents, to which we have referred previously, has been described as providing a *'springboard for curiosity and exploration'*[40] and we know that when children feel secure and safe they engage in these and other learning behaviours including playing, acting on their own initiative, persisting in their efforts and many more. Creating an environment in which the child feels 'at home' appears to be the first step towards enabling children to feel they are safe when they attend out-of-home settings.

When a child feels secure their self-confidence emerges, their personality is evident, their mind is free to imagine, daydream, create, represent and make connections between different experiences; they are already learning. The challenge for practitioners is to ensure that they build strong bonds with parents so that the bridge between the different 'secure bases' of home and school/setting are as strong as possible so that every child feels the ground is firm beneath their feet – every step of the way. It is on this firm basis that the specific areas which we will consider in the next chapter can flourish.

5 Specific Areas of Learning Matter

Aims of the chapter

- To consider the importance of the specific areas of learning for young children
- To identify the significance of Literacy, Mathematics, Understanding the World and Expressive Arts and Design for young children's learning
- To explore approaches to teaching and learning in the specific areas
- To focus on the role of language and interaction in the specific areas

What is important about the specific areas?

Examined separately from the prime areas, which were discussed in the previous chapter, these four areas of learning sound very similar to those which have been traditionally studied in schools by older children. That is because together they create the foundations of subjects that are currently viewed as highly important for children to learn in schools, both in this country and in many other industrialised countries.

There are four specific areas:

- Literacy
- Mathematics
- Understanding the World
- Expressive Arts and Design.

The linkage to school subjects discussed previously is fairly obvious except in respect of Understanding the World which is a repository for the humanities: geography and history and for the sciences including Information and Communications Technology (ICT). The ordering of the specific areas of learning in the revised EYFS (2012) also suggests a hierarchy, however, they have equal status in the learning and development requirements of the EYFS and should therefore be regarded as equally important.

Literacy and Mathematics

The importance of Literacy and Mathematics in life and work, both in the UK and globally, is crucial – especially when these are combined with technological skills. Emphasising this, an interim report by The World Literacy Foundation indicated recently: *'Those people who have strong basic literacy and numeracy skills combined with advanced functional literacy are valuable human capital to their nations and the global economy*.[1] Similarly a report into the costs of poor numeracy skills for children identified five different types of disadvantages that children who had not learned to understand basic number concepts by the age of seven became victim to. These included health and educational costs including more exclusions, the need for behaviour and special needs support, as well as the prospect of being involved in crime or of receiving low wages.[2]

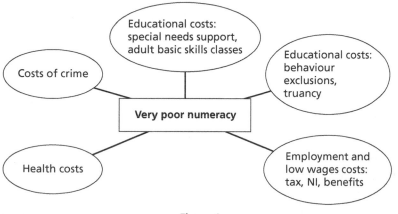

Figure 1

Why literacy is important

Let us consider now the importance of literacy in today's society. Underscoring the findings that poor behaviour causes pupils to be excluded the Centre for Social Justice reported recently: *'Many (children) display challenging behaviour to hide the fact that they cannot read, write or keep up'*.[3] According to a report by the National Literacy Trust 66% of adults believe that being able to read, write and communicate is a fundamental right while 92% of people say literacy is vital to our economy.[4] This is endorsed in a government document which states that *'cities with high youth employment characteristically have significantly lower attainment in GCSE Maths and English'*.[5] While this does not indicate a causal link it does remind us we should make every effort to ensure that children are encouraged to find pleasure in their learning and be taught in ways that ensure they remain 'turned on' to it.

Where jobs are concerned poor literacy skills are also a serious barrier to progress at work and 63% of men and 75% of women with low literacy skills have never received a promotion.[6] Many would argue that literacy is also important because of its power in conveying ideas, giving access to information and transporting us to imaginary worlds. So being literate is important both for itself and for the contribution it can make to an individual's job prospects. However, in an age when printing has never been cheaper and with a plethora of high quality reading materials available through lending libraries, it seems sad that while we are in a golden age of books some 14% of children and young people in lower income homes still rarely read books purely for pleasure.

All of these findings suggest both a widening of the literacy field (as new technologies are accommodated) and a significant change in what is required of today's workforce when being literate is a must while at one time not being literate was less of a problem. Yet when asked about the link between reading and success in work 25% of children and adults did not recognise this connection.[7] While one in six people struggle with literacy in the UK, indicating their literacy is below the expected level of an 11 year old, the situation is rightly a priority for governments, not just in the UK but beyond. It is also vital for settings and schools as well as for parents, all of whom have a contribution to make towards helping all children become literate.

Literacy has been defined narrowly as the ability' to read and write' but in current training materials for school inspectors the definition has been widened to '*include the ability to speak and listen effectively alongside the skills of reading and writing*'.[8] This leads to another important consideration about Literacy and why in the revised EYFS (2012) it has been separated from Communication and Language as well as why each has been assigned to a different group. The broad purpose of the division of the areas of learning has been discussed previously however it is worth mentioning here some related issues.

The roots of literacy start from birth

Firstly if literacy does include the ability to speak and listen then it must be acknowledged that its roots reach back to birth when children begin developing communication skills. Secondly, the skills of reading and writing also start very early as young children encounter books, play with words and sounds, engage with environmental print, listen to and tell stories and make marks on paper and other surfaces.

The first point is important because the separation of Communication and Language from Literacy in the revised EYFS (2012) can be seen as giving precedence to early language skills, recognising the importance of establishing these earlier, rather than later. This is based on sound evidence. At the same time however, while the reading and writing aspects of literacy are not as immediately significant (when a baby is born) they are nonetheless a very large part of children's development and should be nurtured from the beginning, alongside their communication and language skills. Indeed, an important review of reading in England stated '*Obviously, developing children's positive attitudes to literacy, in the broadest sense, from the earliest stage is very important. In the best circumstances, parents and carers, along with settings and schools, do much to foster these attitudes*'.[9] Therefore it is important to stress that while literacy is being discussed throughout this chapter in connection with reading and writing these do not happen in isolation since they are intrinsically connected with communication and language. Let us now consider Literacy in the EYFS.

Literacy in the EYFS

Literacy is set out under two aspects in the revised EYFS:

1 Reading
2 Writing

The learning and development requirements for young children's reading in the revised EYFS (2012) for literacy state that:

> 'Literacy development involves encouraging children to link sounds and letters and to begin to read and write. Children must be given access to a wide range of reading materials (books, poems, and other written materials) to ignite their interest.[10]

Reading
Reading is one of the fundamental skills of literacy that children need to learn if they are to enjoy the pleasures it brings and reap the benefits of being part of a literate society. Definitions of reading are varied but always contain two dimensions: word recognition (decoding) and comprehension (interpretation).[11] It can be

summed up thus: '*Reading is the act of looking at printed words and understanding or comprehending what they are saying, or the act of saying those words out loud or of interpreting those words*'.[12]

The outcomes for Reading at the end of the EYFS (2012) are:

> 'Children read and understand simple sentences. They use phonic knowledge to decode regular words and read them aloud accurately. They also read some common irregular words. They demonstrate understanding when talking with others about what they have read'.

So learning to read is more than simply decoding words on a page because it includes the dimension of understanding the messages conveyed within the words; messages which increasingly become more complex as children engage with more sophisticated texts.

This focus on reading in the early years is not new though current wisdom suggests that reading outcomes should improve as a result of greater knowledge and understanding of this area. However, in spite of this, national data show that reading outcomes have remained relatively static for a number of years. The EYFSP scores for reading in 2011 indicated that 74% of five years old had achieved a good level of development in linking sounds and letters while a slightly smaller number, 72% of children managed to achieve a good level of development in reading. This is not unexpected since there has been an increased focus on the teaching of phonics but what it does suggest is that there is a slight gap between what children know about linking sounds and letters and how they apply or are enabled to apply their knowledge to read and enjoy a range of literature. The learning and development requirements for Reading, referred to above give a very strong steer about how this gap can be bridged since these refer to: '*encouraging children to read …, both through listening to others reading, and being encouraged to begin to read … themselves*' as well as the importance of giving children access '*to … books, poems, and other written materials to ignite their interest.*'[13]

This last statement is pivotal because it gives practitioners a clear message about the importance of sharing books, stories, poems and other literature of the highest quality with children. It would be very easy to overlook this area because it comes at a time of concerns about the phonics screening assessment in Year 1, which we will touch upon shortly. Knowing that the literacy 'menu' we offer to children will inspire them and make them want to read (and write) themselves should give practitioners confidence to focus on literature of all kinds.

This should include access to a range of books by different authors as well as some by the same author – having a favourite author is something most avid readers admit to. Children can be encouraged to be discerning in choosing from so many prolific and distinguished writers including among many others: Julia Donaldson, Michael Rosen, Mick Inkpen, John Burningham, Nick Sharratt, Eric Carle, Nick Butterworth, Janet and Alan Ahlberg, Shirley Hughes, Jill Murphy, Judith Kerr, Tony Ross, David McKee.

Practitioners who add puppets, props such as a toy animal, or a cloak, story boards or sound making materials can further add to the pleasure and excitement. These props can help children to remember parts of the story which interest them or make them tense or make them laugh out loud. Book areas are usually well thought out and presented in the EYFS but in addition books should also be on hand everywhere in the setting so that practitioners and children can find information and stories on topics that are relevant to their interests or at a particular time of the year. Introducing a range of literacy experiences is like immersion in a language: its effects may not be immediately visible but they will begin to show when a child who has heard hundreds of stories sits next to a friend and says: '*Once upon a time ....*' that is a sure sign that a child is immersed in language and is demonstrating that in expressive literacy.

The other building blocks that contribute to the child becoming a reader include '*vocabulary, background knowledge, expressive and receptive language, phonological and phonemic awareness, oral expression* [and] *the alphabetic principle;*'[14] some of these have already been touched on in relation to Communication and Language in the EYFS. Phonological awareness, or hearing the sounds (phonemes) in words, has been shown to be strongly related to reading ability and precedes the ability to recognise printed letters.[15] Phonemic awareness is a more advanced component of phonological awareness involving the metacognitive skills of noticing, thinking about and working out the individual sounds (phonemes) in spoken words and then identifying them, for example: /b/u/g.[16] The alphabetic principle has been described as '*the idea that letters and letter patterns represent the sounds of spoken language. Recognising that there are predictable relationships between sounds and letters allows children to apply these relationships to both familiar and unfamiliar words, and to begin to read with fluency.*[17]

Another clarification which may be necessary is the role of phonics instruction in reading which has been the subject of intense debate in the UK and the US for a considerable time. The simplest advice issued to parents is that:

> 'Phonics is a way of teaching children to read quickly and skilfully. They are taught how to:
> - recognise the sounds that each individual letter makes;
> - identify the sounds that different combinations of letters make – such as 'sh' or 'oo'; and
> - blend these sounds together from left to right to make a word. Children can then use this knowledge to 'de-code' new words that they hear or see. This is the first important step in learning to read'.[18]

This guidance is very important because what is being made clear here is that phonics is seen as the first step in learning to read. Indeed in its arguments supporting the Year 1 phonics screening check the Department for Education argues: 'If children do not learn to read, they cannot read to learn' and because of this it is committed to 'improving the teaching of reading in reception and Year 1 of primary school.'[19]

Therefore during the period of the EYFS, alongside the rich experiences children have of language, story, poems and rhymes, they should also be taught to notice the sounds of spoken language and to hear, identify and manipulate them. As children's knowledge of the sounds in spoken language grows they will (usually) be taught about blending sounds orally for reading (decoding), and segmenting sounds (for writing); writing graphemes which correspond to the sounds heard will also begin. The Independent Review of Reading put it this way: '*Because our writing system is alphabetic, beginner readers must be taught how the letters of the alphabet, singly or in combination, represent the sounds of spoken language (letter sound correspondences) and how to blend (synthesise) the sounds to read words, and break up (segment) the sounds in words to spell. They must learn to process all the letters in words and 'read words in and out of text'. Phonic work should teach these skills and knowledge in a well defined and systematic sequence*'.[20] Since ultimately the '*goal of phonics instruction is to help children to learn and be able to use the Alphabetic Principle,*[21] this teaching should not jeopardise children's enjoyment of reading since the whole purpose of learning to read is so that children can enjoy what it offers and deploy their skills effectively to learn new and interesting things.

Writing

Learning to write is a complex business! Writing is made up of many different processes including secretarial aspects (involving physical skills, discussed in the previous chapter, like gripping and pressing on a pencil) and the compositional elements concerning what to write, as well as the skills associated with identifying the correct grapheme to link with a particular phoneme – such as 'c' to begin writing the word 'cat'. At the same time the writer is involved in reviewing and monitoring what is being conveyed. Neurocognitive functions involved in writing include *'working memory, reasoning, cognition and language'.*[22] The

outcome of all these processes is text generation, which involves creating words, sentences and eventually paragraphs.

As young children talk about and represent their ideas they will, through exposure to an environment in which writing is seen as important, begin to ask about writing, tell adults about their own marks and want to know more about the sounds and letters of the alphabet. The link between the spoken and the written word is often made first when children talk about books with adults and identify features of print such as a book title, or are shown how their own name is written when they want to write it on a card, for example.

From these initial ventures into writing young children need many different types of support to supplement their emerging skills and they may, at times, need adult scribes to write their words. They will also need to see aspects of writing modelled and this will involve demonstrations of the executive functions involved in planning what they want to communicate in their writing as well as being able to observe the conventions expert writers take for granted such as that writing in English goes from left to right and from top to bottom of the page. In addition, they will need to be taught how to form letters in a way that will support their independent, joined-up handwriting in the future.

Describing approaches to the teaching of writing the Early Years Literacy Interboard Group of Northern Ireland (NI) outlines the writing pocess in the NI Foundation Stage. This six stage process begins with:

- 'Familiarisation' to writing, through exposure to many samples of a writing genre followed by:
- 'Problem-solving' which is exploring text genre.

It then recommends there should be:

- 'Modelled writing' (for children) leading to:
- 'Shared writing' (writing with children) and:
- 'Guided writing' (writing with/by children) before leading finally to:
- 'Independent writing' (writing by children).[23]

It should also be noted that the processes above would not necessarily occur in isolation or in any particular order. This is similar to the approach recommended until recently in England by the National Strategies. Their guidance included all the language experiences referred to previously and emphasised the importance of teachers as role models who demonstrate the purposes  of writing, together with children being given opportunities for representing their ideas in ways which initially include mark-making and early or emergent writing.

In the outcomes for writing in the revised EYFS (2012) children are expected to use:

> 'their phonic knowledge to write words in ways which match their spoken sounds.... *[to]* write some irregular common words. *[To]* write simple sentences which can be read by themselves and others' and it is suggested that these will contain 'Some words [that] are spelt correctly and others [that] are phonetically plausible'.[24]

Given the discussion in the previous paragraph and Jim Rose's warning that: 'The teaching of beginners must lead them to understand how reading and writing are related'[25] this is an area which must take as its starting point every child's individual development, particularly focusing on the types of experiences that help young children understand the purposes of writing.

Section review: Why Literacy is important

Thinking

What are the arguments in the previous sections that would persuade you to Jim Rose's view that: *'The teaching of beginners must lead them to understand how reading and writing are related'*?[25]

Reflecting

Consider the following scenario and the sticky notes in the photograph:

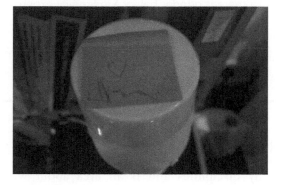

Scenario

> Girl (S): Aged 2 years 6 Months
> 'S' is cared for regularly by her grandparents. One day when she is lifted up to ring the doorbell she is astonished to see a pink sticky note placed next to the doorbell. She asks her granddad, who has collected her from nursery, why the sticky note is stuck on the door and what it says. Her granddad says that it is there because the builders who are working on the house have disconnected the bell from the electricity and that the note says: 'This bell does not work'.
>
> Several days later – a blue sticky note appears on the lamp written by 'S' which she has done without any discussion or help from adults. When asked what her sticky note says she replies: It says: 'This lamp does not work'.
>
> This is the first time that 'S''s grandparents have heard her attribute meaning to her own marks.

What has 'S' demonstrated about her understanding of reading and writing? What does this scenario suggest about a) young children's learning of literacy and b) the contexts in which writing and reading occur?

Doing

- List all the literacy activities that happen that you don't plan for, such as the one described in the previous scenario.
- List all the literacy activities that you plan.
- Identify when and where most literacy learning happens in your setting.
- How do you attempt to ensure there is gender balance in literacy experiences in your setting?
- Evaluate whether you are making full use of every opportunity that arises to develop literacy and what if anything you could do to extend opportunities further.

Why Mathematics is important

Mathematics is fundamental to many disciplines and is an area about which many adults openly express their fear and confusion and about which there has been considerable debate, particularly its importance for people's life chances. A report focused on this area indicated: '*There remains an inherent assumption among adults that being able to deal with numbers and graphics is not as important as being able to read and write competently*'.[26] Yet, it has been shown that while poor literacy and numeracy skills together have a detrimental effect on both male and female employment and their success at work it is women who are more negatively impacted by having poor numeracy skills: making it difficult for them to gain employment, or to function effectively in many areas of life'.[27] This is due, in part, to a rise in non-manual occupations – the balance per head of population in non-manual occupations having changed from 46% in 1971 to 60% in 2010, suggesting the importance in the future for adults to have well-developed numeracy skills.

The world of work seems a long way away from the realities of pre-school and the early years of schooling but clearly, it does have implications for the future of young children since learning is never more rapid than in the early years. We know that under normal circumstances young children: '*develop an everyday mathematics entailing a variety of topics, including space, shape and pattern, as well as number and* number operations'. These include '*informal ideas of more and less, taking away, shape, size, location, pattern and position*'.[28] Unfortunately it is clear from research that knowledge gaps appear in '*large part due to the lack of connection between children's informal and intuitive knowledge and school mathematics*'[29] suggesting that connections are not always made between what children know and what they are expected to learn; a missed opportunity. Furthermore it has been shown that '*mathematics ability upon entry to kindergarten is a stronger predictor of later academic success than is early reading ability*'.[30]

The case for 'mathematizing' or providing appropriate mathematical experiences which are enriched with mathematical vocabulary is strong, according to researchers considering inequities in mathematics education for young children,[31] since it is argued that early mathematical education can help '*children formalise early concepts, make connections among related concepts, and provide the vocabulary and symbol systems necessary for mathematical communication and translation*'.[32]

In a recent review of research into the acquisition of early numeracy skills it was noted: '*There is a difference in opinion about how and when early childhood mathematics (ECME) should be introduced, particularly regarding: a) the amount of structure versus free play and b) specific curriculum versus teachable moments*'.[33] This argument chimes with concerns in this country about the balance between adult-led and child-initiated learning and to some extent is more about pedagogy *per se* than about mathematics particularly. However it is worth consideration since it is an argument that has been explored in some depth by Ginsburg et al[34] who identify six components which they argue should ideally be present in early childhood mathematical education (ECME), visually:

1   Environment
2   Play
3   Teachable moments
4   Projects
5   Curriculum
6   Intentional teaching

A further dimension that Ginsburg stresses is the importance of *mathematical language* since research shows that '*the amount of teachers' math-related talk is significantly related to the growth of pre-schoolers' conventional mathematical knowledge over the school year*'.[35] Without engaging in a long debate about pedagogy here it is worth considering each of the six dimensions recommended by Ginsburg's team in thinking about teaching mathematics in the early years:

Environment – the physical environment should contain 'a rich variety of objects and materials (such as blocks, dressing up area and puzzles) it is important too to remember that the environment should be a space where children feel emotionally confident and where their errors are treated as opportunities for learning.

Play – block play is particularly good for mathematics and children learn a good deal of everyday mathematics on their own, however we are warned that on its own play is not enough if children are to progress in their understanding of mathematical concepts.

Teachable moments – described as adult guidance which involves the teacher's careful observation of children's play and other activities which when accurately perceived and suitably addressed can provide a superb learning experience for the child, though Ginsburg is not convinced that this method is sufficient because of the variation in the quality of interaction.

Projects – described as 'extensive teacher initiated and guided explorations of complex topics related to the everyday world' and involving measurement, space, perspective, representation and many mathematical and scientific ideas these are seen as useful if they do not become 'a grab-bag of any mathematics-related experiences that seem to relate to a theme'.

Curriculum – Ginsburg contextualises projects as being useful if part of a larger plan – namely a curriculum, which is a guide to what is planned for the teaching of mathematics – in England this would be drawn from the EYFS learning and development requirements and informed by Development Matters[36] and the outcomes at the end of the EYFS.

Intentional teaching – this is about the active introduction of mathematical concepts, methods and language through a range of appropriate experiences and teaching strategies which would link to 'teachable moments' and 'projects'.

Figure 2 Ginsburg's model

In identifying how to approach these areas it is important to consider how children learn and the conditions which support their learning and how these correspond to guidance in the EYFS. Consider each of the following statements drawn from the EYFS and their relevance for teaching mathematics to young children:

Play is necessary as a means of learning

- 'Each area of learning and development must be implemented through planned, purposeful play' [because] 'it is essential for children's development, building their confidence as they learn to explore, to think about problems, and relate to others'.

Teaching

- Is a balance between 'adult-led and child-initiated activity'.
- Practitioners must make ongoing judgements 'about the balance between activities led by children, and activities led or guided by adults'.
- Practitioners must respond to each child's emerging needs and interests, guiding their development through warm, positive interaction.

How children learn

- 'Children learn by leading their own play, and by taking part in play which is guided by adults'.
- As children grow older, and as their development allows, it is expected that the balance will gradually shift towards more activities led by adults, to help children prepare for more formal learning, ready for Year 1.'[37]

Putting together these recommendations in the EYFS with those developed by Ginsburg a picture emerges of mathematical pedagogy which should be considered carefully in relation to individual difference and which builds on children's play by introducing a range of approaches which support mathematical learning including:

- An enabling environment for mathematical learning.
- Resources within the environment which are open-ended.
- Developing language and vocabulary to scaffold children's emerging mathematical ideas.

- Selecting 'teachable moments' as well as planning to teach specific concepts and skills when next steps are developed for individuals or groups as part of a curriculum which builds on children's ideas and interests.

Mathematics in the EYFS

The learning and development requirements for mathematics involve:

> 'providing children with opportunities to develop and improve their skills in counting, understanding and using numbers, calculating simple addition and subtraction problems; and *[helping children]* to describe shapes, spaces, and measures'.[38]

At first glance these appear little changed from the EYFS (2007) with the biggest apparent change being the new title: Mathematics which replaces Problem Solving, Reasoning and Numeracy. However this is not the only change: others have been made in response to the EYFS Draft Consultation in 2011. These include the requirement for children to learn about *time* and *money* and *about numbers to 20* (rather than to ten) as well as a requirement to understand *doubling, halving and sharing.*

Mathematics is now presented under two aspects in the revised EYFS:

1 Numbers
2 Shape, Space and Measures

Numbers

Numbers incorporates two aspects which previously appeared separately in the EYFS (2007): Numbers as Labels and for Counting and Calculating. This means that coverage of these will need to be carefully considered so that all the different areas of counting and calculating are addressed over time. The outcomes for this aspect of mathematics are that:

> 'children count reliably with numbers from 1 to 20, place them in order and say which number is one more or one less than a given number. Using quantities and objects, they add and subtract two single-digit numbers and count on or back to find the answer. They solve problems, including doubling, halving and sharing.'[39]

To ensure that this happens successfully it is important to be clear about progression in mathematics and to provide a range of practical activities so that different children can develop mathematical understanding at their own level. A startling finding from research shows '*throughout primary school, curricula and teachers continue to teach children concepts and skills they already know.*'[40] However in contrast another issue, exercising many policy makers at present, is that there are differences between what children with highly developed language skills learn and know compared with children whose language skills do not support them in getting the best from their learning opportunities in settings and schools. To emphasise this point, we are reminded that research indicates that '*Some children have acquired number knowledge before the age of four that other children will not acquire before the age of seven*'.[41]

In order to support children's learning of number it is important for practitioners to be aware of 'developmental progressions' or 'trajectories' in children's under-standing of numbers and of calculation.[42] Put simply this means that the focus should be on understanding the child's starting point and helping the child progress beyond their current level rather than focusing on how to progress through the curriculum *per se*. There is a subtle difference! This is not usually a problem in early years however it should be borne in mind and practitioners should be confident that sound foundations are built by starting with what children know and can do and by understanding any misapprehensions they may have formed about mathematics. We will now focus very briefly on a number of trajectories including subitising, counting, and early addition and subtraction.

Subitising

Subitising has been described as '*the immediate correct assignment of number words to small collections of perceptual items*'[43] or '*recognising a number without consciously using other mental or mathematical processes and then naming it*'.[44] This instant recognition of groups of objects in different configurations '*appears to precede and support the development of counting ability*' and is thought to continue beyond early childhood. The first level of subitising may range from a child of three or four being able to name groups of up to four objects with a corresponding number name, quickly deciding how many stones they have collected or identifying, without counting, the number of apples left over after snack.

Dependent on the individual child's experience they may be able to present a similar number of objects to those they are shown (up to three or four) and to recognise a group of up to four or five objects without counting each one separately. This skill is enhanced by play with 'perceptual patterns'[45] visual patterns such as on a die or dominoes as well as sound patterns where the number of beats or bell rings is known without counting. This ability to develop conceptual patterns leads later to understanding that a configuration of four dots can be decomposed into two and two or considered together to become a set of four. Interestingly a recent report showed that the precision with which pre-school children *'estimate quantities, prior to any formal education in mathematics, predicts their mathematics ability in elementary school'.*[46] According to researchers based at the Kennedy Krieger Institute, more research will be needed to discover *'whether these skills are malleable at an early age, how they contribute to math achievement and if they are related to other known influences on math performance.'*[47]

Counting

Counting is often assumed to be easy – mainly because 'expert counters' such as adults or older children forget how they learned to count. Established by Gelman and Gallistel,[48] there are five principles associated with counting which are:

- The one to one principle: this means that the child must assign only one number to each object in the set.
- The stable order principle: the number words are always in the same order: one, two, three and so on.
- The cardinal principle: the number of objects in the set is the last number word counted: this identifies 'how many' objects in total.
- The abstraction principle: this states that the preceding principles can be applied to any collection of objects, whether physically present or not. These might include sounds, pretend food, or the counting words – as is the case when 'counting on' or 'counting back'.
- The order-irrelevance principle: refers to the knowledge that the order in which items are counted is irrelevant. It does not really matter whether the counting procedure is carried out from left to right, from right to left or from somewhere else, so long as every item in the collection is counted once and only once.[49]

Verbal counting begins with children's knowledge of rhymes and as they learn about things that are important for them, such as their own age. Progression in counting involves learning the number names or labels, reciting them in order and eventually accurately counting an arrangement of objects as well as writing and recognising the associated numerals for the given quantities. This will involve the principles of counting set out above. Progression in counting involves learning the number names or labels, reciting them in order, *backwards and forwards* and eventually accurately counting an arrangement of objects as well as writing and recognising the associated numerals for the given quantities.

Early addition and subtraction

A recent review of early years research indicated that '*Calculation both builds on and draws upon early understanding of number and counting.*'[50] This suggests why the aspects of numbers and calculating have been merged in the new framework since both number knowledge and counting are involved in finding a total – either by joining or by separating groups of objects. This area is often addressed in everyday experiences that practitioners use routinely to develop mathematical understanding as well as in short specific sessions at small group times.

The kinds of experiences that would provide these opportunities could be developed through organising a teddy bear's picnic, planning a celebration or organising a number of 'acts' to do a 'show', or making decisions about the numbers of plants needed to fill a flower bed. In contexts which are embedded in real life experiences children 'get' the purpose of addition or subtraction because it has real meaning for them. Helping children to think mathematically will lead them to identifying and solving mathematical problems for themselves, such as: how to share one apple between two children; how to set out the right number of places at snack time when some members of the group are absent; how to check whether the number of balls in a basket is correct and if any are missing; the skill is in making children 'maths aware'. Planning to develop children's thinking in small group sessions should build on this type of learning in order to connect real experiences with the abstract ideas which will be addressed as children are taught about representing mathematical problems graphically.

Recent Ofsted guidance[51] for school inspectors in the EYFS refers to adults who develop 'numeracy well' – this should alert practitioners to the importance of reviewing the nature of interaction to ensure that when the 'teachable (mathematical) moments' do arrive they are embraced and exploited to ensure that every individual child has their mathematical thinking challenged and makes progress in their learning. In

addition, schools and settings will usually introduce counting rhymes and songs, games, action rhymes and activities as well as encouraging children to use calculation in their play by tallying as well as using numbers.

Further considerations are the type and accessibility of resources to support mathematics. If children are to enjoy mathematics and turn to it readily in their play they should have access to a wide range of materials that support their learning. These might include number lines of various kinds, games, both commercially produced, and developed within the setting and a range of interesting objects to count such as conkers, stones, fir cones, lolly sticks and other items such as apples and coins.

Activities can be modelled by an adult, with teaching input, and then children can be invited to use the same resources independently to explore or practise the mathematical ideas. For example, a practitioner might show children how to make one number into another by adding to or taking away from a group of objects attached to a washing line. Adult: 'There are three socks hanging out to dry – can you make five?' (or seven or two). The purpose of this activity is to *make a new number*. After initial modelling by the adult the resources can then be left out to become a play activity for children who can challenge themselves or one another to make a 'new' number. Encouraging children to think and talk about the operation is important because this will help them to consider the number in the original set and the operation that they have carried out to arrive at the new number. This approach leads to children developing counting strategies that support their ability to count on and back in order to reach a solution to a number problem involving single digit numbers.

In the above areas *'Emphasis should be* [placed] *on meaning and understanding through enhanced discussions'*, rather than on anything else since it is known that *'slow and inefficient learning occurs when principles are not understood'*.[52] As has been discussed in this chapter and elsewhere the importance of language for learning cannot be stressed too highly. We also strongly emphasise the importance of children's learning being embedded in real situations which make sense to them.

Shape, Space and Measures

Shape, Space and Measures links to geometry and to spatial understanding, which are important in other areas of learning as well as mathematics, including design technology, and aspects of Understanding the World. The outcomes for Shape, Space and Measures are:

'children use everyday language to talk about size, weight, capacity, position, distance, time and money to compare quantities and objects and to solve problems. They recognise, create and describe patterns. They explore characteristics of everyday objects and shapes and use mathematical language to describe them.'[53]

Once again it is important to stress the importance of providing an enabling environment in making the different strands of this area relevant, useful and interesting to young children. It is also vital to recognise the connections between different areas of learning which may provide relevant contexts for mathematical understanding. Many activities, such as building a track, comparing heights, or the sizes of the beds needed for the Three Bears are easily introduced in the early years, as are those connected with position and distance – outdoor learning can be particularly good for this aspect because of the added space which makes large-scale work easier.

Volume measurement (capacity), leads to an understanding of standard measures yet begins with a child pouring between measures, identifying which of two containers holds more. Eventually this leads to children counting how many containers of water are needed to fill another such as a baby bath, for example. Another aspect of understanding about volume focuses on how objects, such as building blocks, can fill up a space – a great opportunity for developing this concept would be during 'tidy time' with blocks!

Understanding 'money' and 'time' will be developed most successfully through ensuring that children understand the purpose of what they are doing and that activities are relevant to them. Sand timers, electronic timers and other devices such as stop watches engage children's interest in the passage of time and help them to compare 'how long it took them' to do something. Children love to judge their speed at doing something, such as skipping, riding, or walking and can use timers of all kinds to good effect, eventually recognising that greater units of time need to be measured with conventional clocks, whether analogue or digital.

Money is also best understood in a real context – when children can be encouraged to recognise different coins and to find out about the costs of items. This is more meaningful to a child if they are keen to know how much a toy at a table top sale costs or how much money would be needed to buy a present for a friend. Practice with money is easily addressed in role-play provision whether that is in a shop, post office, café or bank. What is important is that children should have real experiences on which to base their ideas and resources for practical activities including price lists, a cash register, coins, purses, bags as well as clearly labelled and attractive items for 'sale'.

Section review: Why Mathematics is important

Thinking

After reading this section consider how you would develop 'mathematical language' to support children's mathematical thinking in a systematic yet sensitive way, taking account of children's different experiences.

Reflecting

Mathematical trajectories suggest that progression in 'numbers' is incremental. How is planning for mathematical learning underpinned by information from your observations and what do these highlight about individual differences between children?

Doing

Consider the following areas of your provision:

- block play
- home corner
- writing area
- outdoor area
- creative area.

1 Ask adults to focus on ways of promoting children's mathematical language and thinking in each area (as and when appropriate).
2 Focusing on mathematical learning: review or observe adult/child inter-actions in one area for ten minutes over a week (or ask a peer to observe you for ten minutes in several areas).
3 Identify: a) when adults took the opportunity to develop children's

numeracy in any area; b) what contexts led to this; c) whether any area was more exploited in this respect; d) whether any area was not a good place for this kind of learning.
4 Analyse your findings to consider the best contexts for mathematical learning in your setting and the implications of this for future practice.

Why Understanding the World is important

The task for all of us as we move from the confines of our own home and family into a social world is to make sense of the conventions, language, expectations, rules and mores of the place or group we find ourselves in: whether that is somebody else's home or another organisation such as school or work. However the first task for the new baby is to adapt to the people and the place in which s/he is born and to get to know how the social world of the family and the home works. The skills young children have as 'mind-readers' are often discounted yet children as young as four years of age have been shown to infer information about people from very little information. The role of teachers and parents is to help them to build on their powers of inference and deduction so that they do not assess people on the basis of simple stereotypes.

Showing how easily stereotypes are established one experiment introduced two groups of four year olds to a pair of dolls, Anna and Josie which were then able to play on a trampoline and a bicycle. When Anna played she went on both toys happily three out of four times while her companion, Josie, only went on each item just once. Asked by the experimenters to explain the dolls' behaviour one group of four year olds identified that the doll, Anna, showed the trait of 'bravery' while Josie was observed to be 'timid' – they then went on to predict that Anna would continue to be brave in the future. While young children do make inferences about people and their traits the accuracy of their predictions, like the judgements of adults, may not always be correct. Writing about this experiment Alison Gopnik, professor of psychology at the University of California at Berkeley, reminds us that young children may make *profound decisions about someone's character with just a little data*,[54] suggesting that if they are to understand other people children need ways of coming to understand them through such things as stories, poems, plays, role-play as well as through being helped to reflect on their actual relationships with people.

Finding out about other people, communities and traditions is a major part of understanding the world because it also involves asking questions and thinking about the past – this is the beginning of historical enquiry and at a later time leads children to understand that as well as people the place and context of people's lives are important and influence their actions. This can then lead to a consideration of similarities and differences between people and to a wider understanding and concern for other people, the built environment and the natural world.

Understanding the World in the EYFS

The learning and development requirements for this area are:

> 'Understanding the world involves guiding children to make sense of their physical world and their community through opportunities to explore, observe and find out about people, places, technology and the environment'.[55]

As indicated in the previous section young children's judgements of other people are easily influenced – this suggests that misunderstandings about others may arise from misapprehensions or misinformation from other children and adults. This is why it is so important to help young children develop positive self-attitudes since accepting oneself is the starting point for accepting and valuing other people. Best practice in this area suggests that in order to understand the world, a concentric approach is required, beginning with the child, their family, the traditions of the family and the community.

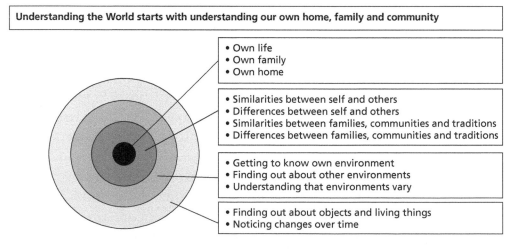

Understanding the World starts with understanding our own home, family and community

- Own life
- Own family
- Own home

- Similarities between self and others
- Differences between self and others
- Similarities between families, communities and traditions
- Differences between families, communities and traditions

- Getting to know own environment
- Finding out about other environments
- Understanding that environments vary

- Finding out about objects and living things
- Noticing changes over time

Figure 3

Children's interests

Exploring, observing and finding out about the world is strengthened when adults guide children's interests, support their curiosity and challenge their thinking as partners in their learning. An example of this is when a child 'brings' from home an interest in something that may not have been 'centre-stage' in the setting, such as a newly acquired family pet, a snake for example. Helping the child to talk about their pet may require the practitioner to improve their own knowledge in order to 'feed' the child's interest and in this process there is a co-construction of learning, with adult and child both learning something new from the other person. In this way the child may be able to discuss confidently the daily food requirements for their snake, while the practitioner may be able to find information that describes different types of snakes and their habitats. This approach will encourage the child to take their learning beyond the 'show and tell' level that otherwise might have occurred and requires planning to be fairly flexible. The benefits are that the child learns that the process of teaching and learning is collaborative, where both they and the practitioner can learn from one another.

The outcomes at the end of the EYFS for children at five years of age in Understanding the World are broad so we deal with these separately in the sections which follow. Understanding the World is set out under three aspects in the revised EYFS which we will now consider:

1 People and Communities
2 The World
3 Technology

People and Communities
Finding out about categories

Young children's learning starts with the particular before they are able to categorise or generalise about properties or groups of objects. For example – the child has a dog at home, Bertie; this particular dog may sum up all dogs to a young child until more dogs come along like Barney and Butcher and Bessie and some other creatures: cats, like Poppy, Petal and Paraguay. Initially the categories are insignificant but eventually the child recognises that 'dogginess' is shared as a category and that just as Bertie is a dog, so too are Barney, Butcher and Bessie – unlike the cats, who while they share some similarities with dogs, are clearly a different animal! The same logic and reasoning can be used by young children to understand the people in their lives and their relationships to one another – beginning first with people that are close to the child before radiating out to people the child knows outside the home or recognises in particular contexts – such as the family doctor or a check-out attendant.

Finding out about people in the community

As children develop an understanding of these networks they begin to understand different roles people play in the community and the jobs people do. This is the beginning of learning about the community and about similarities and differences between people they know. When children are confident in understanding about their own community and its traditions they are able to understand and value others and to celebrate difference.

Children's attitudes reflect what they have learned from other people – influencing children to have a positive sense of their own identity helps them to feel positively towards others: this is the beginning of helping children understand that different people create a community and that people are interdependent and share the world.

The outcomes for People and Communities are:

> 'children talk about past and present events in their own lives and in the lives of family members. They know that other children don't always enjoy the same things, and are sensitive to this. They know about similarities and differences between themselves and others, and among families, communities and traditions.[56]

The World

Although the concepts of similarity and difference are again addressed in 'The World' this aspect contains the roots of geographical and scientific as opposed to social and historical understanding which was the focus of the previous section. In order for children to find out about places, objects, materials and living things they need to have many experiences which inspire their curiosity and allow them to find out about the things that interest them.

Finding out about the environment

One area of interest for young children is the immediate environment of the setting which may be on a busy street, opposite a football ground, deep in the countryside or set beside the sea. Wherever it is located there will be some commonalities such as perimeter fencing, play areas, shops, transport, living things and materials such as stone, brick and wood nearby. At the same time each will have some unique features to explore so a busy street will have lots of street furniture, post and telephone boxes, parking signs, traffic lights, vehicles and shops, while if the setting or school is in the country there will be an abundance of greenery and possibly farm animals, there will certainly be some evidence of non-domestic animals such as voles, hedgehogs and foxes or badgers as well as fences, gates, doors and signs different from those seen in towns.

Finding out about the community

Finding out about the locality is much more fun if children can go out and look at things that interest them: either with their parents or with practitioners. Talking to people whose jobs are very visible to the children such as the crossing patrol attendant, the refuse collectors or the community support team can lead to exciting role-play opportunities as well as to the development of Understanding the World. However there are particular skills associated with Understanding the World which if children encounter early can help them to develop deep level learning. These include:

- Observing: documenting with photographs, drawings, mark-making, writing or speech and video recording.
- Asking questions: such as: 'I wonder where we could find some insects'? or 'What happened to make the soft toy (left out overnight) get so wet, when it didn't rain'?.
- Looking for patterns: patterns are all around us for example on clothes, or in brickwork. Patterns in nature may be less obvious, such as why some plants seem to thrive in some places and others don't. To find answers it may be necessary to observe the garden plot for a while to see where the sun strikes and which plants are in the warmest, coolest, wettest or driest places.
- Classifying: all sorts of materials and items can be sorted to decide what

properties they have in common, for example, whether they float or sink and to identify the common characteristics of a group of objects such as those which can all move because they have wheels.

- Hypothesising: this is a skill we all use and is a bit like thinking aloud: 'I think that ball got to the bottom of the tube because it was heavier than the other ball but I don't know if that's why so I'm going to try a different ball this time'. When practitioners model this approach children learn thinking skills in the process.
- Testing or experimenting: is about trying something out to see the effect of different variables which may lead to discussions about whether paper is always porous and making boats using different strengths of paper, some of which will be more water-resistant than others.

This aspect is intended to lead to the following outcomes at the end of the EYFS:

> 'children know about similarities and differences in relation to places, objects, materials and living things. They talk about the features of their own immediate environment and how environments might vary from one another. They make observations of animals and plants and explain why some things occur, and talk about changes'.[57]

Technology

Advances in technology seem endless and it can be difficult to keep abreast of changing technology. Yet if children are to learn about the purposes and uses of technology it is essential that they have access to devices that are up to date, functional and intrinsically interesting. This in itself is an issue in the early years because of the costs of both purchasing and maintaining the hardware and software and in the upkeep of devices such as interactive whiteboards, PCs or laptops.

Another concern often expressed is that if children are encouraged to use technology they are likely to develop a sedentary lifestyle. This in turn has a number of negative outcomes including poor health and weight gain as well as increasing the amount of time spent alone, none of which are good for young children. All these concerns are worthy of debate. Another issue concerns access to resources since we know from research in the US that ownership of digital media is predominantly within higher income families, though ironically it is children from lower income families that consume the most media.[58]

What is very clear is that computer technology and media use is increasing through popular media platforms including: television, video/DVDs, games consoles, portable music players, smart phones, MP3 players, electronic interactive toys, e-books, PCs, notebooks, laptops and game systems.[59] While there has been an explosion in the number of applications (apps) designed with small children[60] in mind recent research showed: *'that using electronic toys may be detrimental to the quality of parent-child-interaction, and hence fail to assist the early learning goals that parents may have for their children. In three of the four domains of parent-child inter-action explored* (with electronic toys) *it was noted that .... mothers' behaviours were significantly less positive – less responsive, less encouraging, and less instructive'* (compared with their responses in the use of traditional toys).[61]

Given the concerns we have identified it is important that in the EYFS there is a real understanding by practitioners and parents alike of the benefits of using technology, at the same time as there being an awareness of and vigilance about risks.

Finding out about and using technology

In the EYFS we can assume that children will interact with many technological devices and that they can and will develop skills and confidence in their safe use. For the youngest children, this will relate to simple programs on a PC/whiteboard involving click and drag or drag and drop actions – these are also available as touch screen 'apps' and often involve actions such as finding and placing the right clothes on a teddy or a snowman.

Use of a keyboard and mouse are skills which children should also develop – both in simple games and for typing, saving and retrieving their own work, whether that is writing or mark-making in programs such as 'Paint' or through use of a touch screen on an iPad, tablet or an interactive whiteboard.

The use of digital cameras and voice recording items such as 'talking tins', talking albums, talking pegs and talking frames is also very common in the EYFS. These can either be used by the children to talk about their ideas, or comment on their play and learning or they are often used by adults as part of an interactive display encouraging children to try something out, or to follow simple instructions.

Many settings also provide CD players and listening boxes for children to use as part of literacy activities to enable children to listen to stories, sounds and rhymes and songs.

There is also a range of other technology in regular use in early years settings including electronic, and programmable toys such as turtles and Bee Bots which can be programmed to move in sequence. In addition many enhancements and programmes can be purchased or franchised to support children in developing their technological skills.

Using technological tools

In discussions of the use of IT[62] in schools and in response to a review of the National Curriculum the Computing at School Working Group argued that '*IT teaches [a pupil] how to be a thoughtful user of ..... tools*', referring to their use of software in devices controlled by a processor such as programmable toys, phones, game consoles and PCs. National Association of Advisers for Computers in Education (NAACE), which describes itself as an ICT association, representing the voice of the UK education technology community in the schools sector. It sets out five areas for ICT in its draft framework – indicating that there are three key areas: digital life, digital literacy and digital technologies. It then discusses the following areas with reference to the EYFS, though the suggestions which follow are with reference to children from three to five years of age:

NAACE – five areas of ICT

- **Digital literacy** – including online identities; finding information; using ICT to help learning; creating and sharing content and the impact of ICT on our lives.

For example, EYFS children may be observed choosing to use a camera when they think it is appropriate alongside learning. In addition to using the camera to take a photograph and upload it to a computer, they may name parts of the camera which links with technologies and how they work.

In EYFS, children will explore how technology enables us to connect with others.

- **Digital communication** – including online and offline; sharing information; producing media; control; collecting real world data; problem solving and developing confidence and ability to transfer skills.

- **Technology in the world** – including recognising technologies; how technology helps us at home, school and work; introduction to features of web pages; navigating web pages and how technology has changed lives and the world.

In EYFS, children will be supported to make their own images, videos, sound and text content using a range of tools in different contexts. They will learn to communicate with others using different digital tools, e.g. voice recording with microphones built into technology, texting on a mobile phone, picture on an internet page; they will share information about their learning using the same kinds of technology and they may play with floor turtles or other electronic toys, giving them instructions and controlling their movement. In EYFS learners will recognise different types of information on a web page including text, images and buttons to help with navigation. They will develop an awareness of how technology is used in the world around us, including some of the ways people use ICT to help them in their jobs or to make tasks such as grocery shopping more convenient.

NAACE – five areas of ICT

- **Technical understanding** – involving computers and devices containing a computer; technologies store, information (data); programs and programming; networks and the World Wide Web and evolution of technologies.

  In EYFS, children may talk about digital information. In EYFS, children will explore how technology enables us to connect with others. By the end of EYFS, children will have developed an awareness that there is something inside a piece of technology that makes it work, which may be e.g. a code or program in a web page/game or hardware 'bits' inside a DVD player.

- **Safe and responsible use** – involving respect and etiquette; responsible use; online safety; offline safety; health and safety; sharing information and data safely; ownership of information and data and environmental issues.[63]

  EYFS children are learning that appropriate, respectful ways to communicate are important and this should include digital communications, whether online or offline. Knowing that they create things that belong to them and can be shared with others will include the creation of digital artefacts – videos, photos, sound recordings, pictures, etc – and the different ways that technology can help us share with others. This introduces the need for appropriate treatment of information and data. Considering recycling of equipment or turning off the power at night provides a useful introduction to environmental issues.[64]

These areas fit in with current practice in ICT, though they extend well beyond the existing expected outcomes at the end of the EYFS. However, they will be useful in considering how to support children in achieving the outcomes in this aspect, which are:

> 'children recognise that a range of technology is used in places such as homes and schools. They select and use technology for particular purposes'.[65]

At the heart of this process, according to the NAACE proposals, is that children *'need to know what aspects of ICT are available to them, when to use them and why the item they have selected is appropriate to the task'.*[66] Given the speed of change and young children's competence in the use of technology the biggest challenge in this area may well be for practitioners in keeping up with children who do not question the presence of technology in their everyday lives!

Section review: Why Understanding the World is important

Thinking

Understanding the World has many connections to other areas of learning for example: Making Relationships, which is part of Personal, social and emotional development through which *'children learn to take account of one another's ideas about how to organise their activity. They show sensitivity to others' needs and feelings, and form positive relationships with adults and other children'*. What aspects of Understanding the World would link into these areas and how could they both be addressed through the same, or similar experiences and activities?

Reflecting

- Is your current ICT policy clear about how technology is to be used by children in the EYFS – mainly as a tool for communication?
- Given the many concerns which have been raised about the use of technology in the early years how could you develop this area in a way which would ensure that children had opportunities to achieve the learning outcomes while not compromising their safety or their physical and emotional development?

Doing

Audit the sources and uses of technology in your setting – consider some of the following points:

- ease of access in a range of areas
- variety of technological devices: voice recorders, talking books, programmable toys, sound recorders, CD players, electronic toys, smart board, listening stations, PCs, laptops, tablets, iPads etc
- maintenance and upkeep of devices: are batteries re-charged regularly and consistently so that devices are always ready to be used? Is there a regular programme of maintenance to ensure PCs, laptops etc are consistently available?

Why Expressive Arts and Design is important

Creativity and creative potential are frequently areas that can be under-valued in favour of those which are more easily measured. A reason for this may be that these areas are more nebulous and since personal tastes and preferences in the arts often drive us to be more interested in some things than others we can often unintentionally encourage children to share our own interests, rather than help them to identify their own. Whatever our preferences or strengths in expressive arts and design it is likely our provision reflects the things we enjoy more than those which interest us less. Asked to select from the following areas, some 25 course participants, all of whom were female, indicated their preferred areas of creativity in the following order: role-play; art; music; dance; movement; design and technology. Only a handful selected beyond the first two of these areas, suggesting that confidence is not high in the remainder. One reason for this may be that some people have learned that they are not 'good' at particular subjects and so they may not be as open to learning in these areas, nor to developing the skills and potential to encourage others in them.

A major review of creativity, led by chairman Ken Robinson, who has devoted a career to furthering this area, suggested: *'Creativity is possible in all areas of human activity, including the arts, sciences, at work, at play and in all other areas of daily life. All people have creative abilities and we all have them differently. When individuals find their creative strengths, it can have an enormous impact on self-esteem and on overall achievement'.*[67] Unlocking creative potential in young children then does not simply lead to development in one particular area since it widens the individual's learning potential into other areas too, creating a virtuous circle, or a feel-good factor that motivates the child (or adult) to succeed in other domains of learning.

Expressive Arts and Design in the EYFS

Expressive Arts and Design is set out under two aspects in the revised EYFS:

1 Exploring and Using Media and Materials
2 Being Imaginative

The learning and development requirements at the end of the EYFS for this area focus on:

> 'enabling children to explore and play with a wide range of media and materials, as well as providing opportunities and encouragement for sharing their thoughts, ideas and feelings through a variety of activities in art, music, movement, dance, role-play, and design and technology'.[68]

This is quite a wide range, given the different areas to be covered especially since Expresive Arts and Design has been widened to include 'design', previously part of Understanding the World.

Exploring and Using Media and Materials

This aspect is about allowing young children to find out about what sounds, tools and materials can do and what they, in turn, can do with them. The tools, and materials involved will range from mark-making equipment to instruments and pieces of cloth to beautiful stones, or pieces of wood. The techniques children will learn about or develop will depend on the materials: sometimes this will mean children are learning about how to move to soft, flowing sounds, or to sounds that encourage stamping, or creating sounds by banging hard on a drum. At other times techniques may include learning how to use tools such as scissors or large wooden or plastic needles, or finishing the edge of a clay plate with a pattern made by impressing the clay with a fork or a twig.

These techniques are an important part of what artists engage in as they explore and find out about different media such as clay, or paint or through their explorations of character, dance moves, sound and music. It is also important to be aware that explorations often do not involve the creation of a finished product since it may well be sufficient for the person engaged in the exploration to try out a number of processes such as painting on damp paper (as opposed to wet) or exploring a sequence of sounds created by using a variety of materials.

A recent report indicated that teachers thought young children were *'particularly creative because they saw the world in fresh and unconstrained ways.*[69] The difficulty some practitioners have is in trusting the child's creative process, a way to think about this process was proposed by Malaguzzi in discussion of the 'hundred languages of children' when he indicated: *'Creativity becomes more visible when adults try to be more attentive to the cognitive processes of children than to the results they achieve in various fields of doing and understanding'.*[70] In these circumstances practitioners may more often than not find themselves acting as facilitator and resource provider as children carry out such explorations. Sometimes they will need to demonstrate tool use, or support children to develop techniques through discussions with them which allow the child to continue their creative process while figuring out what it is they want to achieve. One key to encouraging the creative process is to consider what it is the child is trying to achieve by finding out about their thinking, through observing them at work. This gives the child time to develop their ideas. If adults are there to support with resources, intervening only when it becomes apparent that the child needs help, or if they ask for an opinion, or if they indicate they have 'finished' the outcome will be the child's. Finished products emerge when, and only when the person who is involved is satisfied with their own process. These exploratory processes are discussed in more depth in relation to the characteristics of effective learning in a later chapter. The outcomes for 'Exploring and Using Media and Materials' are:

> 'children sing songs, make music and dance, and experiment with ways of changing them. They safely use and explore a variety of materials, tools and techniques, experimenting with colour, design, texture, form and function'.

Being Imaginative

Children often have very fertile imaginations, fired by stories, real events and their lived experiences all of which they need to process in order to be able to make sense of them. When we observe children's play we have a perspective on their interests and preoccupations – that is, if children are given time, space and materials to explore. The outcomes for this aspect are that children:

> 'use what they have learnt about media and materials in original ways, thinking about uses and purposes. They represent their own ideas, thoughts and feelings through design and technology, art, music, dance, role-play and stories.'[71]

The important points to note are about using media and materials in '*original ways*' and that what must be facilitated is the development of '*originality*'. Originality is about the ways in which children (and artists) communicate, represent and interpret their experiences, it is fuelled by experiences which 'feed' the imagination, which may take time to 'incubate' and which may be developed over time. Craftspeople often spend much of their time drawing and/or representing their ideas in different ways before creating a product and in that process may produce line drawings, or plans which show details of different parts of a product before they ever reach the final stage of production. Introducing this way of working to younger children ensures that they understand that as well as involving 'one-off' products' creativity is at times a multi-layered process which evolves over time, as different ideas, feelings and reflections are brought into the mix.

A sobering statistic from the US is that in spite of children being viewed as highly creative this attribute is not maintained throughout childhood since '*creativity (as measured by divergent thinking tests) declines when children enter kindergarten, at around the age of six*.'[72]

To encourage children to develop originality it is important for adults to be open-minded and non-judgemental about what children produce – indeed imagination is identified as one of four processes in creativity: '*Imaginative activity is a form of mental play – serious play directed towards some creative purpose. It is a mode of thought which is essentially generative: ….. Creative insights often occur when existing ideas are combined or reinterpreted in unexpected ways or when they are applied in areas with which they are not normally associated. Often this arises by making unusual connections, seeing analogies and relationships between ideas or objects that have not previously been related*'.[73] How many early years practitioners see this in action on an almost daily basis: water added to sand, glue added to paint, sticky tape and lolly sticks lovingly woven into a necklace – the list is endless. What should be avoided is children learning to evaluate their own or others' efforts and endeavours as not 'good' enough. The creative process is a journey – not all paths take travellers where they want to go. However, by helping children to keep an open mind about their ideas practitioners can help children to appreciate their own creativity.

Art and Design

The only limits to artistic development are those connected with resources and imagination in the main and, fortunately many early years settings abound in both. Children are naturally interested in mark-making and drawing using materials such as crayons, pastels, chalks, markers and pencils. They also enjoy enhancing their work by adding to it using wool, string, beads, shiny materials, pieces of fabrics and found materials. Modelling with clay, and straws and making models from a range of items such as cartons, tubes, cardboard, corks and bottle tops appeals to children. Initially models may be randomly created but eventually planning what is to be made will include making simple drawings of an item or talking about what is to be made: this is the beginning of design technology.

Music, Movement and Dance

Moving to music is as natural to children as breathing – even small babies move rhythmically when they hear sounds and babies of eight or nine months will bob up and down to singing, clapping and rhythmic sounds. Dance is a natural progression from music and *'is thought to foster healthy development in a wide variety of domains, including self-image, self-body awareness, and self-esteem; coping with emotional and cognitive challenges; concentration and focus; tolerance and respect for diverse others; emotional expression and understanding; tension relief and emotional release; self-control; problem solving, decision making, taking responsibility, making adjustments and adaptations and testing alternatives.'*[74] However, until recently, while these claims had been made, there was little research in this area, though there is now a greater interest. Nevertheless some supporting evidence of the value of dance comes from research conducted with children aged between 39 and 62 months in a Head Start programme some of whom took part in an eight week session of structured movement activities. These children were encouraged to continuously invent movements while a randomly assigned control group followed normal play activities. It was found the 'movement' group made significant gains in their social skills at the same time as achieving significant improvements in their self-management (behaviour) over the course of the program, whereas the children not exposed to the dance program showed little progress in either measure.[75] Another piece of research carried out by Sacha and Russ with pre-school children using the concept of imagery to help children visualise movements or ideas (such as jumping over a pile of imaginary leaves or reaching out to allow a pretend bird to light on their hand) found that compared with children in a control group the visual imagery group took less time *'to master the skill, and showed'* [better] *'long-term recall and prompting, initial attentiveness, and long-term enjoyment'.*[76]

Role-play

The area where young children often feel least constrained is role-play, pretend or imaginative play in which reality is suspended and anything is possible. This can sometimes involve stories, parts of stories or ideas children bring with them to the setting from television programmes or other experiences. Creative practitioners can support children's play through the thoughtful provision of open-ended resources as well as through offering suggestions that support children to take their ideas forward. The value of such play has been shown to be an important area with a *'growing body of evidence supporting the many connections between cognitive competence and high-quality pretend play. If children lack opportunities to experience such play, their long-term capacities related to metacognition, problem solving, and social cognition, as well as to academic areas such as literacy, mathematics, and science, may be diminished. These complex and multidimensional skills involving many areas of the brain are most likely to thrive in an atmosphere rich in high-quality pretend play'.*[77] In an overview of research on children's play the author describes play as 'world-making', stating: *'During play, children built whole worlds using their own materials, space, time and imagination.'*[78] Expressive arts and design is an area that could easily be left to chance – it is important to ensure that it is valued because it is fundamental to children's creative development and underpins learning across many areas.

Section review: Why Expressive Arts and Design is important

Thinking

Which of the following areas is easiest to plan and provide for? Which is the most difficult? Is there a gender bias in any strand?

- Art
- Music
- Movement
- Dance
- Role-play
- Design and technology

Reflecting

How do the opportunities and experiences on offer in your setting contribute to children developing non-stereotypical views of the expressive arts and design? What else could you do to ensure that young children see themselves as 'artists' who are encouraged to express their ideas, thoughts and feelings through a range of media?

Doing

Analyse the range of activities and experiences you currently provide that support children's development in Expressive Arts and Design.

Identify whether within these there are opportunities for children to re-visit and take further their creative processes, for example:

- Have children been able to record their music-making, re-play it and add to it making new variations on their 'original' composition?

- Have children discussed ways of developing their pictures by thinking about the background and foreground in, for example, a scene depicting the sea?
- How do children learn about extending dance and movement routines, and adding to these incrementally?
- How do children learn about the processes in design and technology? Are there opportunities for them to 'draw their designs' in the workshop area and to discuss their thinking about problems and solutions they may have to overcome to make something functional?

Conclusion

In this chapter we have considered the four specific areas of the EYFS, which together with the prime areas, form the basis of the early years curriculum from September 2012 in England. In doing so we have emphasised the importance of language in learning since we believe that language underpins children's conceptual understanding. While communication and language, one of the prime areas, focuses on this we also believe that the language associated with each of the EYFS (2012) areas of learning should be enhanced so that children can clarify their thoughts, name or label objects, communicate their ideas and develop higher order thinking skills.

We believe that adult role models also influence children's learning since it is they who inspire and enthuse children, and become the listeners or resource providers who help them to develop their interests from day to day and week to week.

In this role and through their interactions with children adults help them develop the confidence to try things out for themselves, not to be put off when things don't turn out as expected and to develop a love of learning that will continue throughout their lives. They do this because they have learnt that success is about the process of learning not about acquiring an ill assorted bag of facts which have no meaning for them.

Every child can enjoy learning and can experience success – the best influences they can have in schools and settings are people who understand them, who become companions on their very different and diverse learning journeys and who are creative and playful themselves.

6 Environment Matters

Aims of the chapter

- To consider an enabling environment in the EYFS
- To explore the importance of partnerships between parents, practitioners and others
- To identify ways the environment can be responsive to children's individual needs, particularly through the role of the key person
- To identify how environments and resources can support children's learning in the EYFS

In previous chapters we have discussed the way children develop and the areas of learning in the revised EYFS. In this, and subsequent chapters, we consider the areas that significantly influence children's learning in the EYFS beginning here with a brief examination of how and why the environment matters in the EYFS before considering the roles of play, interaction, the home and pedagogy in learning in further chapters.

The term 'an enabling environment' has slipped into common usage in England since the introduction of the EYFS in 2007 and in spite of moves to substitute it for something simpler and more accessible it has survived and is retained as a principle in the revised EYFS (2012). The principles are described as '*shaping practice in the EYFS*' – though few words have been used to elucidate how this might happen, we are told: '*children learn and develop well in enabling environments, in which their experiences respond to their individual needs and there is a strong partnership between practitioners and parents and/or carers*'.[1]

This suggests that central to an enabling environment are two main strands:

- experiences which meet and are responsive to children's individual needs
- partnerships between parents and practitioners.

This is a good starting point though these conditions would not be sufficient alone and should be considered in relationship to the three remaining principles which are:

- A Unique Child: *'every child is a unique child, who is constantly learning and can be resilient, capable, confident and self-assured'*;
- Positive Relationships: *'children learn to be strong and independent through positive relationships'*;
- Learning and Development: *'children develop and learn in different ways and at different rates. The framework covers the education and care of all children in early years provision, including children with special educational needs and disabilities'*.[2]

What is most striking about the principles above is their focus on the uniqueness of the child and the importance of relationships for children's development and learning. In essence, when they are put into practice, the principles partially describe an ethos or philosophy which underpins the EYFS. The part that remains and is not expressed is developed uniquely by leaders and managers and by practitioners who are in daily contact with parents, children and others whose work or skills bring them into the setting, such as members of the community. We will now consider what we believe to be some of the different dimensions of an enabling environment in the EYFS.

An enabling environment – partnerships

When a child attends a setting at any age they remain psychologically connected to their family. The first and most important thing to consider is how to ensure that the setting enables parents and carers to feel involved and part of their child's experience in the setting. This can sometimes seem problematic either because: there is a lack of physical space to accommodate parents or carers; there are time constraints experienced by busy parents; some parents may be perceived as being either not willing or not able to engage with the setting. These are barriers which can seem insurmountable yet not all may be real and not all may be permanent. If parents recognise that the setting has an 'open-door' policy and that practitioners are non-judgemental and supportive these barriers can often be overcome.

Developing sound partnerships of any kind can be a lengthy and complex business and like any relationship they are built incrementally as each partner learns to trust the other. Many wonderful relationships have been built by such partnerships where parents who were children themselves in a setting return to it with their own children – confident that this place will do the 'right' thing for their child. Sometimes relationships are strengthened when a particularly challenging circumstance arises: perhaps providing additional support for a family during a period when a parent is hospitalised, or working with the parents to meet the particular needs of a child. The lengths to which many settings will go to ensure partnerships are built between themselves and parents whose children attend the setting are truly remarkable. We have seen this reflected in many testaments as diverse as Ofsted reports to letters and cards from grateful parents.

Unless ground rules are established early however, one or other partner can be left feeling unclear about the parameters of the partnership, particularly when things don't run smoothly. Therefore it is important for settings to develop policies which are understood by practitioners and which are shared with parents from first contact so that ambiguities do not creep in about the setting's commitment to the family and child or the family's responsibilities relating to the child while they attend the setting. This is normal practice in the majority of early years settings but can sometimes be overlooked when this 'contract' is developing in the initial stage of pre-attendance visits. Among the many areas that will be addressed, the most important are set out in the EYFS Safeguarding and Welfare Requirements[3] but it will also be useful to consider introducing the following:

- An expectation that there will be regular communication about the child's development and learning.
- The importance of parents being involved in their children's learning.
- An expectation that the setting is keen to improve their communication and will treat feedback from parents as helpful information that will shape the setting's development.

Some of the areas cited above are routinely achieved; some are more challenging to achieve. The basis of all of them is in developing positive relationships through the leadership and ethos of the setting and through the key person system.

An enabling environment – social and emotional development

The role of the key person, to which we will return again in a later chapter, is fundamental in supporting children socially and emotionally, whether they work with a five month old baby or a five year old child. This is made clear in the revised EYFS (2012) where it states: '*The key person must help ensure that every child's learning and care is tailored to meet their*  *individual needs. The key person must seek to engage and support parents and/or carers in guiding their child's development at home. They should also help families engage with more specialist support if appropriate*'.[4] It is then indicated that: '*Their role is to help ensure that every child's care is tailored to meet their individual needs, to help the child become familiar with the setting, offer a settled relationship for the child and build a relationship with their parents*'.[5]

These statements are unequivocal and underscore the importance of the role of the key person in supporting the child and in working with parents as partners.

The key person approach is very well established in many settings, particularly those with babies and younger children, and it is seen as a very successful conduit for listening to children, communicating about individual children and for making links with parents. The success of this approach is supported by systems which provide opportunities for professional discussions between practitioners and managers or leaders about issues arising and lessons learned from feedback. Many settings demonstrate in their self-evaluation documentation the ways in which the key person approach works. Exceptionally, some settings allow children to identify their own key person, based on the child's preference, others allocate children and adults to groups, while in a very few the role of the key person may not be fully embedded. Common sense, if nothing else, should tell us that where young children are concerned the most important thing we can do is to provide an emotional 'meeting point' with somebody who has their best interests at heart. That is the role of the key person: an ambassador, who negotiates the terrain for each child in their care. Settings which provide for this are learning communities: the best settings for young children.

An enabling environment – physical spaces

The environment comprises all the physical spaces children encounter within it, whether indoors or out of doors; places to eat, sleep or play. The environment for learning is often thought about in terms of play spaces and, dependent on the ages of children, is often set out in areas of provision which are intended to support the child's learning and development. This will include emotionally, physically, socially, linguistically, and mathematically together with their self-expression; their attitudes to learning and their development of skills such as relating well to others, understanding the world and the community and reading and writing.

The word 'rich' is in danger of becoming hackneyed in discussion of environments for early learning but it acts as a reminder that if the environment is to work effectively it needs to grab children's attention, absorb their interest, inspire their curiosity, provide a stimulus for their learning and offer materials and resources that engage them safely. Many settings are extremely successful at providing enabling environments that do these things, allowing even the youngest children access to materials and resources which they can reach independently or with very little help – from mud kitchens to duck viewing platforms!

The arrangement and layout of spaces is important in this respect because these provide a backdrop for the type of learning that the space can accommodate. Many settings use a limited colour palette to create a calming environment, substituting natural materials for brightly coloured items. Personal preference and the building itself influence such choices – there are no hard and fast rules. The most important thing is that the space should work for the setting and the children and the adults who spend time in it.

Creative use of space often means that even the smallest, apparently unimportant bits of space are used to create areas for children to explore and enjoy. We have seen small spaces beneath cupboards developed into areas which small children can crawl into and outdoor areas which have been enhanced with old trees made into benches, picnic tables, stepping stones and stages and we have seen decking with balustrades developed as building sites full of sand, wheelbarrows and real spades – spaces children can't resist! The imagination of practitioners is often unbounded and resources are frequently used innovatively to create provocations for children's learning. Take the massive tubes from carpet rolls that some settings provide, or the wonderful structures created by fixing together lengths of wooden guttering to allow children to create channels and water falls – there are many more. The more open-ended areas can be, the more a range of learning is likely to take place within them because children can use spaces and resources for their own purposes.

An enabling environment – outdoors

Outdoor spaces can offer the same materials as indoor spaces though some would argue that the difference in scale between the two may offer different possibilities as we discussed earlier in relation to mathematical learning. However the development of outdoor spaces should be as rigorous as for indoor areas, indeed these can offer different perspectives since they look out to the world beyond the setting where children can observe natural as well as manufactured artefacts.

If outdoor provision is developed in the same way as internal space there will be places where children can be quiet and detached from the central areas of action, where they can talk, look at books, or listen quietly; or where they can make marks or draw or paint. There will also be places where they can move vigorously and make a lot of noise and where they can run, jump, roll, climb and balance. There will be spaces too where they can care for, touch and smell different plants in addition to places where they can play with water, sand, pebbles, twigs, clay and chalk, as well as places where they can make music and sound and dance to sounds they have created. There is no better adventure playground than an outdoor area which entices children to explore to hide, to find, to imagine and to play!

An enabling environment – children's learning

It is not our intention to describe how the environment should be created: other books have done that ably. However we know that when the conditions are 'right' children choose to play and when they choose to play they are primed to learn. What helps them to take steps in their learning is the involvement of reflective practitioners; adults that engage with them in a variety of ways. This may be as an observer, a facilitator, a resource provider, thinking or talking partner or a collaborator in the play – some of the pedagogical tools we discuss in more depth later in this book.

When the environment is set out with children's learning in mind it may look radically different from one setting to another. Many settings help children to re-visit their learning by providing space for their partially completed products. Reflective practitioners provide the stimulus which motivates children to go back to what they started earlier, by talking to them about their processes and helping them to think about what else they might want to do – whether that is to develop a piece of writing, a picture, a model, or a construction made from blocks. Using this approach, the practitioner is scaffolding the child's learning, providing opportunities for them to talk about their ideas, thoughts or feelings.

An enabling environment – resources to support learning

When the environment is prepared and the resources are easily accessed children can be encouraged to learn how to care for and return resources to where others can find them. If the environment and resources create a space in which children can develop independence this frees up adults to follow children's interests and encourages children to develop their ideas in some depth because they know that they will be given time to pursue them.

Creating and selling resources has become a huge and fascinating market – with many resource providers standing out from the crowd through thoughtfully engaging with children, pre-schools, schools and practitioners, as well as parents, to identify the effectiveness of their resources and how they can be used. Some resources can support learning wonderfully, for example those which encourage children to make sounds and music – whether these are beautifully crafted semi-permanent features of the environment or a string of pans on a fence will be down to the individual setting and their budgets! Many of the things that children want to play with are available for little or no cost: water, shredded paper, sand, mud, stones, sticks, logs, conkers, twigs, bubbles, clay, string, soft wire, pipe cleaners and pegs. Enhancements for these can be more costly but offer children possibilities to explore their personal agendas whether these are about re-living the experience of a birthday party – with mud pies and twig candles, or of making a machine to fly to the moon.

Making the environment work in the EYFS is essential because at its optimum level it can provide not only physical spaces and resources, but an ethos in which learning is nurtured through emotional support and high quality teaching, based in interactions through which the child's interests are accommodated and extended and in which the involvement of adults who are playful yet skilful enables children to become independent and capable learners.

7 Play Matters in the EYFS

Aims of the chapter

- To elaborate the close connection between play and learning
- To consider the role and function of play in babies' and young children's learning, in both the original and revised versions of the EYFS (2007, 2012)
- To explore the notion of a play-based curriculum with the youngest and oldest children in the EYFS
- To explore relevant issues that measuring outcomes presents, with particular reference to assessment through the revised EYFSFP.

The place of play in early childhood education has never been more contested than now when, in the revised EYFS, it may appear a much greater emphasis is being placed on the outcomes rather than the processes of children's learning. That is not to say that references to play are omitted from the revised EYFS (2012), rather that its role in learning is given less discussion in the leaner version of the framework. As a result, a strong justification for the role of play in early learning is essential if early childhood education is to demonstrate both how and why play matters in the EYFS.

This chapter sets out to elaborate the intimate connection between play and learning, showing that by focusing on the processes involved in play positive outcomes are more, rather than less, achievable. It does so firstly by considering the role and function of play in babies' and young children's learning, it then focuses on the place of play in both the original and revised versions of the EYFS (2007, 2012) before examining examples of playful pedagogy, leading to an exploration of a play-based curriculum with the youngest and oldest children in the EYFS. It will also explore relevant related issues that measuring outcomes presents, such as the problems of assessment through the revised EYFSP. Finally, our aim is to engage the reader to think about how the issues presented will affect their current practice and to prompt their reflection on the value of play so that they feel confident to develop new directions for future action.

The purpose of play

It is important to define and understand babies' and young children's play and the role of play in children's development.

Picture a three year old girl with her own roll of sticky tape. It is New Year's Day and she is not using the sticky tape in the way you or I would use it: she is running delightedly ahead of the roll as the sticky tape unravels behind her, sticking itself to everything it comes into contact with, including the floor and the door, before it wraps itself round her legs. Momentarily she is thrown forward, at this point the adults around her are poised to remonstrate with her, in order to protect her from harm, rather than spoil her fun. Indeed there is confusion about whether she should have the roll of tape at all. But within a moment she is off running again this time stopping in amazement as the last bit of the tape is unleashed from the roll and with a great whooshing sound it gathers itself into a muddled heap behind her as the tension is released: 'It's like a great big party popper, it's like a great big party popper' the three year old shrieks time and again with delight, falling to the floor laughing out loud. So is this play? If it is how do we know? Would we want children in pre-school settings to be doing what this three year old did, we may wonder, as we perhaps shudder at the thought of the expense of all that sticky tape being used up to no purpose when our budgets are at rock bottom.

In search of a universal definition of play, Gwen Gordon, a creative consultant, who began her career creating muppets for Sesame Street, suggests that the search for a universal definition of play is *'pure folly'*,[1] while Robert Fagan, a leader in studying animal play goes further arguing: *'The most irritating feature of play is not the perceptual incoherence, as such, but rather, that play taunts us with its inaccessibility. We feel that something is behind it all, but we do not know, or have forgotten how to see it'.*[2] Clearly something was behind the play of our three year old she was having fun, finding out what happens when you unravel a roll of (cheap) sticky tape, unconventionally trailing it along the floor as opposed to using it to fix things together, amazed and delighted when it mimicked the sound and trajectory of a party popper, catapulting from her hands then falling into a sticky heap behind her. We conjecture she is perhaps connecting previous experience of a party popper, seen at a Christmas party? So what *is* behind it all?

In a review of the connection between play and learning the following definition of play is proposed: *'Play is often defined as activity done for its own sake, characterised by means rather than ends (the process is more important than any end point or goal), flexibility (objects are put in new combinations or roles are acted out in new ways), and positive affect (children often smile, laugh, and say they enjoy it)'.*[3] This is helpful for two reasons – firstly because if we go back to our three year old with the sticky tape it perfectly matches what was described: the activity was done for its own sake, the process involved finding out what could be done with the sticky tape; the sticky tape was being used in a new way; there was positive affect – she laughed and shrieked with delight when the 'party- popper' sound was made. Secondly it provides us with clear criteria for assessing play *per se,* which allows us to distinguish it from other activities such as work, which has a definite goal.[4]

So what, if any, purpose is there in play and what role does it have in children's development? Play has many purposes and its role in young children's development appears to be far-reaching. Many studies suggest that play in 'juveniles' (the young of a species) is functional both at the time it takes place and because of its contribution to future adaptability which supports the juvenile's survival into adulthood. This is because play is believed to afford *'opportunities for behavioural and cognitive innovation and subsequent practice of newly developed behaviours and strategies'.*[5] This explanation suggests play provides the developing child (or animal) with a way of understanding their 'world', or 'niche', through offering them a safe means of exploring a range of behaviours, relationships and ways of being.

In a discussion of play and learning Hirsh-Pasek supports this view concluding that: *'play is a central ingredient in learning, allowing children to imitate adult behaviours, practise motor skills, process emotional events, and learn much about their world'.*[6] The transition from childhood to adulthood is a lengthy period in which, when babies and young children play in safe or familiar environments, provided they are free from stress, they find out about themselves and the world through interacting with people and objects and through their appropriation and use of objects and mastery of language. So practitioners may ask whether children can go it alone, and be left to get on with their play, without the help or involvement of adults. To explore this question we will shortly consider the status of play in the original and revised versions of the EYFS focusing on how play and learning are seen to be connected.

Section review: The purpose of play

Thinking

Play is one of the things that many people 'know' is right for children. From your reading of this section consider the evidence which supports the value of young children's play and how this could be expressed by practitioners feeling under pressure to engage in more formal teaching of young children.

Reflecting

Should there a distinction between the types of play which are acceptable in a group setting? Would you, for example allow a child to use up a small roll of inexpensive sticky tape for no 'useful' purpose? Why? Why not?

Doing

Observe an adult-led and a child-initiated activity in a part of a setting where you don't usually work using Smith and Pellegrini's criteria of play:

  1 An activity done for its own sake.
  2 The process is more important than any end point or goal.
  3 Objects are put in new combinations or roles are acted out in new ways.
  4 Children often smile, laugh, and say they are enjoying themselves'.[7]

Consider to what extent the criteria are met in each activity. Identify the value of each activity in terms of children's learning. What are the benefits of each?

The place of play

We can consider the place of play in the original and revised versions of the EYFS focusing on perceptions of play and learning. In exploring the role and place of play in the original EYFS (2007) Dame Clare Tickell affirmed '*The EYFS currently includes a requirement for the areas of learning to be delivered through planned, purposeful play*' ..... stating: '*I support this focus on play .... It is clear from the evidence that play helps young children to develop the skills they need in order to become good learners – for example helping children to develop flexibility of thought, build their confidence, and see problems from different perspectives*'.[8] This position was subsequently retained in the draft consultation which followed, though reference to the value of play was considerably lost, particularly since it indicated: '*This will move increasingly towards adult-led learning as children start to prepare for reception class*',[9] the underlying assumption apparently being that the purpose of early education was seen as preparation for later learning. Not surprisingly, strong arguments to the contrary subsequently led to a re-think of this position, with the DFE affirming: '*The EYFS framework* ...... *recognises the central importance of play in children's learning*',[10] (though this did not any sense imply an abandonment of the view that the EYFS should contribute to children's readiness for school, a debate we shall continue to explore).

Positively, however, after assurance that there was to be a '*clear and strong emphasis on play as an essential vehicle for children's learning*':[11] particularly '*playing and exploring*'[12] the revised EYFS framework (2012) states: '*Play is essential for children's development, building their confidence as they learn to explore, to think about problems, and relate to others. Children learn by leading their own play, and by taking part in play which is guided by adults*'.[13] However what is notable is that play is rarely discussed, in either version of the EYFS documents, without a corresponding reference to activities initiated by children, and activities led or guided by adults. This leads back to perceptions about the value of play and whether it is seen as being educative as well as how adults (as 'teachers') are expected to support children's play so that their learning is enhanced. This links to a school readiness agenda, suggesting that on its own play is considered insufficient for learning.

In expanding on a theory of play Sutton-Smith, a highly influential figure in the field, indicates that we should be careful about approaches to school readiness warning us that: '*Despite the opposition of the reading-writing-and-arithmetic Puritans with their no-child-left-behind 'work-ethic' programs, the contemporary world needs to be aware of the layers of ludic duality (the complexity of play) involved in forming the minds and mental health of the very young*'.[14] So is it possible that in their desire to prepare children for school adults might abrogate children's play, transforming it to suit their purposes, rather than allowing children to retain their own? Conversely if they don't engage with children in their play are they missing opportunities to invest in this powerful vehicle for learning? These are some of the questions about pedagogy and the adult's role in children's learning which we will address in the next section and further chapters of this book.

Section review: The place of play

Thinking

From your reading of this section consider the place of play in the revised EYFS together with the 'readiness for school' agenda, referred to in this chapter and in Chapter 1. How, in your view, can the two positions be reconciled?

Reflecting

Changing direction can be difficult in any organisation and carrying on as before can seem to be safe, yet if we accept that the EYFS has always been a play-based curriculum could the re-statement of this in the revised EYFS (2012) offer an option for change in your setting?

Doing

Planning to change the balance of activity in your setting to include more play may be supported by assessing your play provision. Using a blank copy of the hexagon below, record what proportions of sessions or days are made up of the following elements for a child, or group of children:

- children's free or independent play/child-initiated activity
- adult-led activity.

Think about an hour's session comprising six ten minute periods or a day comprising six hours, approximately. In the following example two ten minute segments in an hour-long session have been completed.
- Analyse the balance between children's free, or independent play and adult-led and child-initiated activity.
- Decide if this concurs with the focus on play in the revised EYFS.

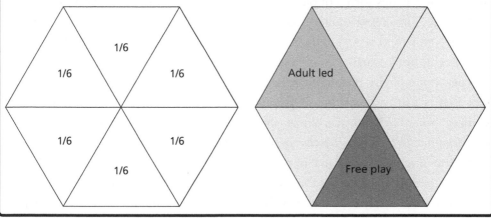

A pedagogy of play and playful learning

In helpfully providing a resume of the role of play in the original EYFS the Tickell Review also identified a common problem, visually that: *'there is confusion about what learning through play actually means, and what the implications of this are for the role of adults'*.[15] This confusion reflects earlier debates in this chapter about what play is, whether it has a useful role and whether by engaging with children when they are playing adults cause the play to end and 'non-play' to begin – this has been described as drudgery[16] in some of the literature, while interestingly Piaget argued that when children play they are, in fact, working.[17]

Some settings advocate children's independent play as the purest (and best) form of play because it meets criteria showing there are few or no external constraints since it is extrinsically motivated, freely chosen, and non-literal, in addition to it actively engaging the learner and being pleasurable.[18] The confusion that Tickell identified comes at a time when there is increasing concern, particularly in the US, about children's play being endangered[19] due to concerns which include a greater emphasis on their dependence on electronic entertainment; a rising focus on the teaching of literacy and numeracy in kindergarten programmes; in addition to an increased amount of time spent in sports and other organized activities for young children, leaving little time for their own play activities (many similar anxieties are echoed in the UK). Concerns raised about children's loss of well-being through too much structure include those of a doctor, Alvin Rosenfield,[20] who, writing for parents of young children, discussed the dangers of an 'over-scheduled' childhood; while the US Surgeon General also warned of over scheduled 'free-time' leading to increasing concerns about children's mental health.[21]

Reconciling these positions, a number of influential researchers have begun to consider the various forms of play which are frequently identified, adding to them 'guided play',[22] involving adults. This category differs from the types of play discussed elsewhere and represents attempts to re-position arguments about the benefits of play for children's learning, the researchers pointing out *'that there exists a false and counterproductive dichotomy between play on the one hand and learning on the other'*.[23] It is to this definition of guided play we will turn in discussing play and learning: *'where children actively engage in pleasurable and seemingly spontaneous activities under the subtle direction of adults'*[24] to explore what playful pedagogy and playful learning might look like in practice.

Playful pedagogy suggests that teaching and learning is a stress-free process; what it does not imply is that it is without any kind of outcomes. One explanation supporting this view of play (with 'learning outcomes') is that the play of babies and young children (up to about the age of two) is so intrinsically linked with their development that it is often indistinguishable from their exploratory behaviour, their communicative and social development, and the physicality of their bodies (motor development).[25] This play/learning continuum is of course enhanced by the contingency of a caring adult who extends the baby's interest and their willingness to play, with interventions such as:

- *'making clown faces at the baby*
- *making ... babbling noises in the baby's face*
- *blowing raspberries on the baby's body*
- *pedalling the babies legs*
- *poking out a tongue at the baby'.*[26]

Here we see the playful 'pedagogue', or adult, leading the baby's play, though of course quite quickly adults also learn to follow the lead of the baby or young child. Indeed, if early years educators were to add up all the 'pretend cups' of tea given them to 'drink' by children in their settings they would quite probably all qualify for a free detox programme!

Playful interventions in children's play and learning with a slightly older age group might involve 'scaffolding', or supporting, a child's thinking by identifying, through discussion, the objects needed to successfully weed an overgrown piece of ground, for example; or, answering questions posed by a curious child such as: *'who came to the party?', 'why is it dark?', 'where do bubbles go?'*. Playfulness in responsiveness is neither patronising nor demeaning to the child; it simply reflects openness and a willingness to support the child to reach new understandings. In discussion of Vygotsky's view Hughes; Abbott & Langston and others, refer to 'scaffolding' which occurs when the adult works with the child in the zone of proximal development (ZPD).[27][28] Hughes describes the ZPD as being the distance between what the child can do alone compared with what he or she can do with support. That is, the child's actual performance, contrasted with his or her potential ability in a different social context. This suggests that if we ask the child to work alone on solving a problem, for example how to protect the bird food from squirrels and other animals s/he will *'display a particular level of performance'*, which does not reflect his/her true performance and that with the support of a more knowledgeable adult (or child) *'she might perform at a higher level than when working alone'*.[29] In this way the child will potentially reach a different conclusion because of receiving new information, or considering issues which s/he might not otherwise have taken into account. The child will have learned something from the interaction with the adult; even if s/he decides his/her own solution is better than the adult's solution.

Section review: A pedagogy of play and playful learning

Thinking

From your reading of this section consider ways in which adults in your setting work with children in the 'ZPD'. Is this something that is discussed between practitioners or is it a taken-for-granted activity that is just 'done' by everybody?

Reflecting

If all learning doesn't just happen what implications are there for the role of practitioners as *'subtle guides'* of children's play? If adults guide or 'scaffold' children's play are they taking over children's play or are they supporting children's learning? Is this likely to be problematic philosophically to 'purists' who believe children have an entitlement to play freely?

Doing

For several whole or part sessions over a one week period try to follow the lead of a child or a group of children, allowing yourself to suspend expectations of the outcomes of these sessions.

Keep brief notes and/or examples of any new or unexpected lines of play children have followed. Analyse:

a) whether anything changed in terms of relationships with children
b) what, if any, issues this produced in terms of 'coverage' of the EYFS areas of learning.

Having established that the process of play and learning is integrally linked to children's development we will go on to consider how a curriculum that is play-based can support children's learning outcomes in the EYFS.

Supporting children's learning outcomes in the EYFS with a play-based curriculum

A significant concern throughout this chapter has been on elaborating the intimate connection between play and learning, highlighting how by focusing on the processes involved in play positive outcomes can be more, rather than less achievable. We now turn to consider how a curriculum based on play can lead to the learning outcomes set out in the EYFS. Many claims have been made for the benefits of play for children's learning these include enhancing emotional, social and personal development, literacy,[30] numeracy and creativity among many others. In a concise scrutiny into the benefits of play it is indicated that *correlational and experimental evidence suggest important benefits of play*.[31] The areas selected in that review link to the types of play discussed previously in

this chapter. A useful example given is in relation to socio-dramatic play which we are told: '*can involve understanding others' intent, sophisticated language constructions, and development of (sometimes) novel and intricate story lines*'.[32] Taking this argument further with reference to the role of symbolic play in literacy it is argued: '*The very nature of symbolic play (first-order symbolism) has an intimate relationship with reading and writing (second-order symbolism) in that children use a similar representational process in both*'.[33] So, on the one hand, when a child uses an object, such as a block, as a telephone, they know it is not actually a telephone, and although they know (at some level) that the block is just a block, while it suits their play scenario the block becomes a telephone. Later, in a different context, it may be used conventionally as a block to build a structure.

As we have discussed in a previous chapter, the system of symbols in reading and writing requires a similar, though different level of understanding: the letters which represent the sounds that are used in making words are symbols which alone are meaningless, but in the context of the written word they become meaningful and can be manipulated both to create and enter other worlds. Using marks and known symbols is at the heart of early writing and decoding. Making meaning from symbols is the basis of reading – so the child who asks *'what does it say?'* may have little awareness of the alphabetic code but is certainly aware that print carries meaning: one of the steps towards becoming a reader.

Phonological awareness, which is sensitivity to sounds in spoken language, is another strand of literacy involved in breaking the alphabetic code. This occurs as children play with real and nonsense words in rhymes, songs and jingles: for example, a child may repeat phrases and words they have heard – just enjoying the rhyme of saying: *'gently Bentley'*, or *'upsy Daisy'* or the tone of *'Run, run as fast you can, you can't catch me, I'm the gingerbread man!'* It is noteworthy that symbolic play such as has been described is *'an often over-looked important scaffold to literacy'*[34] and it is significant that, as with many complex processes, the benefits of such play may not be immediately obvious but are nonetheless a necessary part of children's emergent literacy.

Another report, this time related to mathematics, revealed that *'Babies show numerical competence almost from the day they are born,* [And] *children enter the world prepared to notice number as a feature of their environment'*.[35] Similarly in a naturalistic experiment on children's mathematical development researchers found that through play children build concepts about mathematics in relation to pattern and shape, comparison (magnitude) and enumeration (judging quantity).[36]

Returning to the EYFS it is clear that different enabling environments can provide children with opportunities for building on their interests in numbers and calculating and in shape, space and measures through stories, physical activity, exploration, singing, rhymes, talk and access to materials. In addition to providing these stimuli it would seem that the task of the educator is to enhance children's learning, building on the mathematical knowledge children bring with them to the setting, through guided interaction such as we have previously discussed.

Other areas shown to be developed through play are personal, social and emotional behaviours such as self-awareness, and self-regulation, alongside social and emotional understanding of others. This sense of being a person with thoughts, feelings and preferences is enhanced not only through interactions with adults but also with peers. So the development of friendships (through playing with others) is highly significant for young children since these support them in developing empathy and care of others as well as themselves.

Peer interaction and increased language and communication skills take the young child beyond solitary and parallel play, creating endless possibilities for play in which narratives are explored and stories transformed. Here, in a few words, a leader can challenge a follower to join in a spontaneous play episode: '*I'm not Goldilocks, you're Goldilocks, you have to go a long walk, don't you, then you come to the cottage*'. The response from the chosen child can go one of several ways: they will play Goldilocks (at least for a while); or else they will select a preferred role, or they will decide not to play at all. Whichever outcome occurs both children are learning from the experience.

So what are the children learning from this type of interaction? They are finding ways to relate to one another – part of Personal, Social and Emotional Development. In the process of their play they are finding ways to manage their feelings and behaviour since inevitably the competition for taking particular roles is often intense and one of the players may be disappointed in the role they have to play, yet the fact that they join in with the play demonstrates that they are managing their feelings.

Section review: Supporting children's learning outcomes in the EYFS with a play-based curriculum

Thinking

From your reading of this section, consider how the EYFS prime areas of learning could be developed through pretend play in your setting.

Reflecting

In order to nurture children's spontaneity schedules may need to be flexible. How can flexibility be built into routines to ensure that organisational influences don't encroach on children's opportunities for spontaneous play?

Doing

Identify any learning outcome you think important for children in your group. Find and provide three different ways of helping children to achieve the outcome. Ensure at least one of the ways is completely play-based such as for example providing a range of palettes, paints and different sized brushes and mark-making implements to facilitate children's exploration of media. Compare the nature of adult-child interaction in each of the three sessions and identify the amount of time spent by children in each. Draw conclusions from this about the benefits of play.

They are also listening and attending to their partner in play and recalling the story as well as speaking and listening and using their imagination(s). It is clear that even in such a brief play agenda a great deal of learning is going on – the art of pedagogy is in respecting children's choices and in recognising that the quality of their learning relies on the provision of inspiring experiences, activities and resources that provoke children's interest. Playful pedagogy is about skilfully nurturing and enhancing children's spontaneous interests so that they retain a sense of awe and wonder about the amazing world which is beneath them, around them and within them.

Assessing children's learning in a play-based curriculum

A difficulty which emerges when play leads learning is how to catch it happening since confusion has often arisen in the past because of over-prescription about recording observations, making assessments and moderation of the EYFSP. The revised EYFS framework makes clear that practitioners should observe and respond to each child in their care on an ongoing basis. Therefore while there is no real change in this area one difference that may occur is regarding assessment, where we are advised: '*Paperwork should be limited to that which is absolutely necessary to promote children's successful learning and development.*'[37] This will mean that practice in observation will need to be streamlined. This leaves practitioners with the puzzling dilemma of judging what is sufficient for the purposes of observation-led practice when only a minimum of paperwork should be created. A way round this, which is increasingly followed, is for practitioners to be involved in participant observation – this requires skill and practice yet is invaluable in that it creates exactly the right conditions for ongoing assessments to be made.

When adults are involved in children's play they are supporting their learning – this gives them a window into the child's world and allows them to make judgments about children's current levels of attainment and their progress. Take a practitioner working with an 18 month old toddler who is interested in imitating the adult as s/he writes a list. The child wants the pen and the paper yet his/her skills in mark-making are not proficient in using a pen, since it has little surface area which makes it difficult to establish a good grip on it. The skilful practitioner accommodates the child's desire to imitate her/him by patiently positioning the paper and showing the child how to exert enough pressure on the pen so that the child will see something visible for their efforts. In the moment of this encounter the skilful practitioner has not only been 'teaching' the child they have also been observing and making ongoing assessments of the child's interests and levels of development. Doing this is relatively easy: recording it is often the difficulty. One method many practitioners employ to make a useable record is to make a copy of the child's marks and annotate it – though only if this is a significant event for the child's development, rather than an everyday occurrence. Another method is to take a photograph which is annotated later, a third way is to jot the information on a sticky note to add to the child's file.

Ongoing, daily assessments of children will continue in the revised EYFS in the same way as previously. These will be used as the basis for establishing a child's current level of development and learning and to identify 'next steps' for individual children. If we return to our 18 month old child we can see that the possible lines of development for this child may lie in many directions: the practitioner may focus on encouraging other possibilities for imitating adults that appeal to the toddler such as setting the table at lunch time; wiping surfaces or sweeping the floor – activities many young children love to be involved in. Alternatively the practitioner may recognise the previous behaviour indicates that the child will enjoy other mark-making opportunities and provide a range of these. In this way observation will inform her ongoing assessments, which in turn will inform practice and will ultimately shape what is offered to the child.

Summative assessment

Summative assessment for the two year old check will require information about a child's development across all the eight aspects of the prime areas of learning. This should not require any more paperwork than previously, indeed it may prove to be less demanding since progress in the specific areas is not formally reported on until later. In completing the 24 to 36 month's progress check for a child it will be important to have examples of observations such as those described above, as evidence of progress, (or lack of it). If a child is not progressing in any of the prime areas plans should show how the setting is addressing this – so for example it may be clear that the 18 month old child is not beginning to attempt to say words such as 'gone' when the pen has been put away, in this case discussions with parents will have taken place and the setting will show how they are sensitively working on developing this area with the family and the child.

The second point at which a summative assessment of children's development and learning takes place is at the end of the EYFS. This area will be clarified further when the Standards and Testing Agency (STA) publish the arrangements for assessment in the revised EYFSP. It will be important that this recognises that practitioners have the professional skills to make valid judgments about children's learning.

Section review: Assessing children's learning in a play-based curriculum

Thinking

After reading this section, consider the systems that are used in your setting to make informed judgments about children's development, their play and their progress. How do you keep documentation to *'what is absolutely necessary to promote children's successful learning and development?'*

Reflecting

A child who chooses what to play with may be working at a higher level than when involved in an activity chosen by another person. What, if any issues does this raise for assessment practice in your setting?

Doing

For settings working with children up to the age of three:

- identify how children's play supports their development in the prime areas; what measures could be put in place to support children's play if there were any concerns about a child's development in these areas.

For settings working with children from three to five years:

- review whether current assessment procedures focus sufficiently on play and on recognition of children's achievements demonstrated through play.

Conclusion

In this chapter we have touched on some of the important issues that practitioners face when they provide a play-based curriculum in the EYFS. As has been noted, play is a complex process which is sometimes not fully understood because it is difficult to define and because it appears messy and disorganised. If it appears that way then trying to observe and assess children's development and learning can seem difficult too. Similarly it may feel at times that the art of providing for play is also hard to pin down. Yet in reality it is about trusting in children since *'almost all children play, except those who are malnourished, deprived, or have severe disabilities. [And] Between 3% and 20% of children's time and energy is typically spent in play'* ..... [if] *'young children are deprived of play opportunities, for example being kept in a classroom they play for longer and more vigorously afterwards'.*[38] On this evidence alone it would suggest that under normal circumstances children have a disposition towards play. This suggests that play is functional to their development and that it serves a vital purpose, providing them with opportunities to encounter the world first-hand using their growing repertoire of thought, language, memory and reasoning to understand it, learn from it and to find a way of being in it.

Every child is unique – this is not only a principle of the EYFS but a scientific fact – every child brings something different to their play and takes something different from it – that is the capacity of the human spirit which has led to such magnificent creativity and invention in the world. If we want children's play to be beneficial we would do well to hold on to these thoughts: children are playful; play can lead to high level learning; learning can be fun; and that while the evidence tells us children can learn through formal instruction (and often do so at certain times) children learn best under conditions which allow them the time and freedom to explore. This is summed up in the following lines:

'1) Children need both unstructured free play and playful learning under the gentle guidance of adults ...;
2) academic and social development are so inextricably intertwined that the former must not trump attention to the latter; and
3) learning and play are not incompatible; learning takes place best when children are engaged and enjoying themselves.'[39]

The EYFS is a play-based curriculum – the skill of the practitioner is in making play and learning fun and providing a balance between the two so that through skilful pedagogy, which we explore in a later chapter of this book, children's play leads to learning and ultimately to the required outcomes at the end of the EYFS.

Interaction Matters: Positive relationships

Aims of the chapter

- To focus on positive relationships and the significance of interaction in the EYFS for babies and young children
- To explore the role of the key person in interaction
- To consider the impact of the quality of interaction on children's learning and thinking

In this chapter we consider the importance of interactions. We discuss how relationships between adults and children build social and emotional skills from an early age. This is often viewed as a 'dance' and helps to build the bond of secure attachment. This leads to a discussion of the role of the key person, a vital role for professionals and retained as a legal requirement in the revised EYFS framework. Our purpose here is to consider how the role of the key person offers many opportunities for quality interactions between adults and children. We then consider communication and language and discuss how these are pivotal to relationships, as well as thinking and learning. The chapter concludes with a range of practical strategies from which to build a base to develop quality interactions with children across the EYFS.

Building secure emotional attachments for babies and young children

One of the four guiding principles in the revised EYFS, and retained from the 2007 version, is that children learn to be strong and independent through the interactions they have with others. Positive interactions between a caring adult and a child build important social and emotional skills from an early age. Young children learn to understand their emotions and how to regulate them through relationships with other people, which is the first step in becoming securely attached. Attachment is having a lasting emotional tie to a particular person. Babies and young children quickly become resilient and develop confidence if they have support from caring adults. Early interactions with parents and carers typically take place when a child is being held, during feeding or when the child is in discomfort. A baby cries to have its basic needs met, it is hungry, or thirsty or cold and the adult responds by feeding or soothing. Even in this brief interaction, the child experiences positive emotions which build a bond between the adult and the child and helps construct the emotional architecture of the growing brain.

You might like to think of attachment fostered through interactions as a 'relationship dance' that takes place between a parent or carer and the child. It gives children a sense of who they are and the place they occupy in the world. It communicates to some children, 'I can do this. I am capable and confident'. For others, the message is, 'I am scared because the world is an unsafe place to be'. Young children do not have a sense of their own identity but caring interactions with people around them create this very quickly. Babies form attachments with more than one person, usually the mother, father, grandparents or a practitioner but they develop a stronger attachment with at least one person who is usually the baby's main caregiver and the one the child spends the most time with. According to developmental psychologists the first few months of a baby's life are most important for the development of attachment.[1] It is during this time that parents attune to a baby's signals and sounds and where the personal relationship grows.

Stages of attachment

For children up to the age of two years three stages of attachment were proposed by attachment research pioneer John Bowlby[2] in the 1950s, with a further stage after that age.

Stage 1 called 'Pre-attachment' from birth to two months is where the baby responds to any other person.

Stage 2 from two to seven months is the 'Attachment-in-the-making' stage where the baby recognises and responds well to the main caregiver, who in turn responds affectionately.

Stage 3 is 'Clear-cut attachment' in the period seven to 24 months. In this period the child protests when the parent leaves and there is a wariness of strangers.

Stage 4 is from 24 months in which the child recognises the needs of the carer and makes adjustments so that the relationship and the emotional support can continue.

Interactions support building attachment with babies in a number of ways, for example:

- by breastfeeding, if this is possible
- picking the baby up, smiling at them and talking to them
- using 'motherese'[3] (this term describes the features of adult-baby talk that comprises simplified language with fewer words and grammar structures, incorporating pauses and emphasising certain words). This is a common approach taken by parents and an important part of adult-child bonding.
- rocking a baby gently to soothe and comfort
- gentle massage.

At six months babies turn their heads in the direction of voices and react to their name. Responding to the baby's gazes encourages them to smile back as does looking directly at the baby. At 12 months, children respond to their own reflection in a mirror. They enjoy close contact with adults and give and receive hugs. Giving lots of affection and praise is also extremely important as is reading stories and singing songs: playing simple games like peek-a-boo and those with copying actions. Playing with the baby and following his or her lead is also essential.

At 18 months, children are curious about other people and some may be shy or anxious with strangers. They dislike changes in everyday routines and show mood swings from excited to unhappy quickly. Explaining to a child if the daily routine has to change helps prevent anxiety developing. By 24 months children show determination but also frustration. They test how parents respond to different behaviours, show a wider range of feelings and imitate adult behaviours. Although they may be shy or anxious with strangers they form close attachment with a parent or carer. Encouraging a range of emotions, and language to express these, helps babies and children to express their own emotions.

For children aged three to five years, meeting the social and emotional needs of a mobile toddler and a verbal pre-schooler requires increasing parenting and caring skills. Parents and carers need to be sensitive to the individual needs of the child and understand how to use language to reason with a child, in their interactions. They need to control their own emotions and manage each developmental stage confidently.

As children move through the stages of attachment they develop independent judgment and negotiate relationships with peers and adults.[4] From two to three years, children use their developing mental capacities to interpret experiences and understand what others are thinking. They have a greater range of emotions to draw upon and improved language skills to communicate their feelings. Because of this they are better placed to manage everyday social interactions with peers and with adults. Psychologist Laura Berk[5] tells us that 'emotional intelligence includes perceiving emotions accurately, expressing emotion appropriately, understanding the causes and consequences of emotions, and managing one's own and others' feelings to facilitate thinking and social interaction'.

Positive interactions and warm and loving relationships between adults and children lead to approximately 70% of children aged under 18 months showing secure attachment. Children who make strong attachments cry less when separated, they engage in more pretend play, are less prone to attention deficit problems and can control their personal feelings. They are less aggressive, are at a lower risk of being bullied in school and are popular with peers and adults.[6]

Young children experience their world as an environment of relationships. The quality and stability of a child's early relationships lay the foundation for a wide range of developmental outcomes – better self-confidence and mental health, motivation to learn, achievement in school and later in life. It brings the ability to control aggressive impulses and to resolve conflicts in non-violent ways, knowing the difference between right and wrong, having the capacity to develop and sustain friendships and intimate relationships, and ultimately to be a successful parent oneself.[7] Interactions with peers and with adults can develop all of these. This is the 'serve and return' interaction we described earlier in the book in which young children's body language, their speech sounds and later language are responded to by a caring adult. This creates a safe environment and one in which a child can feel confident.

Supporting secure attachments in the EYFS

Effective practice in the EYFS will provide individual children with opportunities to develop a positive self-concept, interdependent relationships and a personal identity. In order to do this for babies it is suggested that,[8] *'the sort of acceptance that babies and young children need from parents and other important people is not acceptance that is dependent on their behaviour; it is acceptance without reservations and without judgements. It can be described as 'unconditional positive regard'*…Babies learn that they are acceptable by experiencing, day by day, the results of that acceptance…when 'an *'important person' smiles at the baby, and when that person comes at the baby's call, the sense that he or she is acceptable is confirmed. This is not simply a passive process; all the time the baby is learning by experience how to win the smiles, how to bring the person. Every experience is a learning experience.'* The key person relationship is crucial in promoting secure attachment. This role is covered in two places in the revised framework for the EYFS:[9]

- In Section 1, The Learning and Development Requirements, where the requirement is; '*1.11 Each child must be assigned a key person (a safeguarding and welfare requirement – see paragraph 3.26). Providers must inform parents and/or carers of the name of the key person, and explain their role, when a child starts attending a setting. The key person must help ensure that every child's learning and care is tailored to meet their individual needs. The key person must seek to engage and support parents and/or carers in guiding their child's development at home. They should also help families engage with more specialist support if appropriate.'*
- In Section 3, The Safeguarding and Welfare Requirements repeats some of the text from Section 1; '*3.26 Each child must be assigned a key person. Their role is to help ensure that every child's care is tailored to meet their individual needs (in accordance with paragraph 1.11), to help the child become familiar with the*

> *setting, offer a settled relationship for the child and build a relationship with their parents.'*

The Safeguarding and Welfare requirements have been revised and updated in ways that clarify and simplify some of the previous requirements, but the simplified description of the role of the key person gives practitioners little additional information on how they must work with children and their families as they implement the revised framework.

Much of the detail of relationships between each key person and the children they work with has been relocated in the new version of Development Matters,[10] the non-statutory practice guidance.

This document provides very helpful and well-structured guidance for practitioners working with children at each of the six developmental stages. It also moves the detail of practice for the key person into a much closer relationship with the requirements for learning and development. Practitioners and their managers should be aware that in removing the detail of the key person role from the Statutory Requirements, the unique nature between individual children and their key person may become diluted.

The series of cards which formed an essential part of the original EYFS pack (2007) is still recommended reading for practitioners and should be used alongside the revised documentation. Among these, the card giving guidance on the role of the key person (2.4) is particularly useful, giving examples in all the essential areas of the key person role: Secure attachment; Shared care; Independence; and Effective practice.

Section review: Building secure emotional attachments for babies and young children

Thinking

There are ten key emotional needs:

- Attention
- Acceptance
- Appreciation
- Encouragement
- Affection
- Respect
- Support

- Comfort
- Approval
- Security

Consider each of these in turn. Think how interactions in your setting or classroom support each of these needs in babies and young children.

Reflecting

Good relationships underpin all aspects of development and learning identified in the EYFS. Good interactions are the vehicle to promote them. How do staff interactions in your setting or class support relationships with all children?

What strategies do you use to ensure that babies feel secure and form close attachments?

Refer to your copy of the Key Person card from the original EYFS pack (card 2.4). Read and reflect on the examples given in the section on Secure attachment, and consider how you can maintain these as you implement the revised framework.

Doing

How do you and staff in your setting or school build into their everyday interactions with children the communication of emotions? Do you acknowledge these emotions even at times when it is difficult for you personally?

How do you develop a shared understanding with parents and other adults of these emotions?

What do you do when behaviour is challenging and yet still maintain a trusting and caring relationship with a child?

Use the Challenges and dilemmas section of the Key Person card to help your discussions.

The essential role of the key person in the revised EYFS

The best way to foster positive relationships in settings is through the key person approach. There is a statutory duty in the welfare requirements[11] of the new EYFS framework that each child must be assigned a key person (see table opposite). The purpose of this role is to help ensure that every child's needs are met, by helping the child become familiar with the setting, offering a settled relationship for the child and building relationships with parents. Providers must inform parents of the key person's name and explain the role to them when a child starts to attend a setting (in childminding settings, the key person is obviously the childminder themself). The key person must help ensure learning is tailored to meet individual needs and they must engage and support parents, helping them to connect with more specialist support if appropriate (see Section 1.11 Statutory Framework). In the EYFS, this important role requires professionals to be 'tuned in' to individual children to understand how meeting the needs of a two year old or a five year old are different and call for different types of interaction.

For babies who spend much of their early life in settings, rather than in the home, the relationship between a baby and a key person is especially significant. Babies need time to foster these important relationships, time to learn to be independent from a base of loving and secure relationships with their key person.

The role of the key person in reception classes is a more complex one, requiring commitment and planning by practitioners and their managers. The pressures in schools are different from those in pre-school settings, and the adult-child ratios, combined with the increasing pressures of the more formal curriculum often adversely affect the time and commitment for the key person role. However, as described in the following example from a school, this continuing statutory requirement can be fulfilled, offering continuing support to individual children and their families in the first year of statutory schooling. This summary has particular

The requirements	A named member of staff who has more contact than others with the child	Is someone to build a relationship with the child and their parents/carers	Helps the child become familiar with the provision	Meets the child's individual needs and care needs (e.g. dressing, toileting)	Responds sensitively to the child's feelings, ideas and behaviour
Examples of practice	• Dedicated time for key person groups on a regular basis. • Practitioners spend time in the Continuous Provision with key children regularly. • System for allocation of key person.	• Plans and delivers workshop on key person for parents prior to child entering setting. • Informs parents of their key person. • Key person attends home visits/ settling in visits with child and meets parents. • Key person has time dedicated to getting to know parents/carers. • Key person has dedicated time getting for to know child – e.g. plays with child, talks, observes, listen to, involves in games /activities. • Key person informs parents of time at setting via verbal or written feedback at regular intervals. • Invite parents to share lunch. • Invite parents for story time led by key person. • Key person delivers Family Learning Sessions.	• Key person visits child's previous setting to ascertain general experiences prior to attending setting. • Key person uses this knowledge to try to make the new provision welcoming and familiar to child. • Key person has dedicated time for working in the provision with children.	Key person is available to support children with toileting and dressing for as long as the child needs. Arranges gradual introductions to playgrounds and lunch halls where key person can support children if needed. Key person understands child development and contributes to co-ordinate of their learning journey/next steps for planning. Key person observes children regularly and discusses this with other colleagues and parents to move the child on.	Key person has appropriate information about the child to enable them to do this, e.g. position in family, any behaviour patterns, friendship groups, SEN, medical conditions etc Children are able to communicate with key person to enable them to share their ideas and feelings in a way that best suits them. (One to one time, group time, use of resources, etc). Key person delivers PSED focused regular sessions (e.g. circle time) to encourage social and emotional development in a supportive environment.

reference to reception age children, and was provided by a colleague in a recent training session with teachers.

The role of the key person in promoting children's social and emotional development through quality interactions and meeting the requirements of the EYFS is one that requires a variety of personal and professional skills from practitioners. The role is an important one: *'Infant attachment is critical, both because of its place in initiating pathways of development and because of its connection with so many critical developmental functions – social relatedness, arousal modulation, emotional regulation, and curiosity, to name just a few. Attachment experiences remain, even in this complex view, vital in the formation of the person.'*[12]

Section review: The critical role of the key person

Thinking

Think about different times of the day and consider what interactions take place in the key person role in your setting:

- at snack times
- first thing in the morning
- saying good bye
- toileting
- getting changed
- rest times.

Reflecting

Read and reflect on this short case study.

Cassie is 36 months old and has recently started at her local nursery. Staff have observed that she appears indifferent to the adults and is not at all bothered when her mum leaves her every day. She shows no preference between adults she knows and strangers.

Sophie, her key person is concerned that Cassie rarely smiles and does not engage in play activities. She has also observed that there does not seem to be a close relationship between Cassie and her mum.

What would you advise Sophie and the staff at the nursery staff to do to ensure that Cassie's needs are met? What advice would you give to help improve the quality of interactions?

> ### Doing
>
> In your role as a key person for a group of children in your setting. Keep a daily diary for one week. Note the interactions you have with children. When did these take place during the day? Where did they occur? Who initiated them? How did you as a professional develop the interactions?
>
> If you work in a reception class, make some brief notes of the interactions you have with your key children. What do these observations tell you? How does your role compare with the example of the key person in reception given above?

The role of the key person in supporting communication and language development

Communication enables babies and young children to exercise control over their worlds and is at the heart of social interactions for these social beings. Communication is a combination of non-verbal messages that are both given and received (such as body language, gestures, facial expressions and eye contact) and verbal communication through speaking and listening.

From birth babies are ready and eager communicators: they use their senses to understand the strange new world around them and respond to what their senses tell them. In her book *Babytalk*,[13] author Sally Ward reminds us that newborn babies arrive helpless and dependent and yet equipped in a number of ways to interact with adults. They show an emotional inclination towards people and soon engage in the process of communication. In the first month their responsiveness to adults is shown by being quieted through eye contact, when spoken to and by being picked up. Early cries and vocalisations are not yet used to communicate intentionally but the adult nonetheless responds, 'Oh you want your nappy changed' or looking at a nearby toy, 'You want to see teddy' and bringing it towards the baby.

By six months, the baby responds to different people, is aware of strangers and shows shyness for the first time as well as awareness of peers through smiles and vocalisations. By 12 months they integrate interactions with objects and people and will pull an adult's sleeve and point to an object. Their intentional sound-making has increased and it is now much easier for adults to understand exactly what they want to communicate. First words are heard by the first year. Participation in play is more active and baby and adult participate on equal terms in games that build up language through repetition and rhythm. Babies love to listen to the familiarity of nursery rhymes said by an adult and turn-taking games set a child of this age on the road to becoming a conversationalist.

By 24 months, understanding and use of language has really taken off. Conversation is well established, with some increased understanding of what other people know and there is a rapid expansion of vocabulary over the year. Language is used in a variety of ways: babbling is less and the child is keen to tell others about interesting events. We hear more questions, 'Who dat?' and the use of negatives in speech, 'No drink'. Two word sentences are common. If you work with two year olds, you will recognise that children of this age demand others to engage in conversation with them. By three, the drive to be independent is still present. When conversation partners do not understand, the child repeats what was said and is now able to change what was said to help the partner understand meaning better. By four, the child understands a range of verbs, adjectives and prepositions and uses more complex grammatically correct sentences. The child has more strategies to begin conversations, such as 'Do you know.....?' and is more aware of the conventions of conversing such as knowing when a question is being asked.

Communication through verbal and non-verbal channels is the basis through which language is developed. Language is the foundation for children's interactions with other people and provides a vehicle for expressing their needs, thinking and their experiences. One author[14] tells us that to develop communication skills children need to want to communicate. They must have a social interest in what is going on around them. Children need secure affectionate relationships with adults who motivate them to communicate and who provide feedback on their communication. As we have just described, the role of the key person is an ideal one to foster communication. Young children need many interaction opportunities with familiar and unfamiliar adults and with their peers in order to learn about cultural and social conventions, to learn what appropriate social interaction is and support communication skills such as initiating, responding, greeting, requesting and taking turns. They need opportunities to interact with adults to hear spoken language and understand it to use their developing expressive language. At home, everyday events become important times for language learning for babies: bath times, nappy changing and feeding provide ideal opportunities for them to hear language and learn about its structures and vocabulary. In settings that really do promote and value communication, enabling environments are filled with language so that all children can become immersed in words, rhythms and sounds.

As children grow, imaginative play alone and with other children, play with toys, clothes and everyday objects, sharing books with an adult all extend this further, providing ideal contexts to practise and apply their developing language skills and to support cognition and social understanding. In the REPEY project,[15] the quality of adult-child interactions was identified as the key feature in settings rated highest where children made most progress. What was observed were the episodes of co-constructed learning between children and adults. This is what Bruner referred to as a 'joint involvement episodes', where both parties enjoyed being with each other and sharing a joint activity. There are many examples of these throughout the project, many of which were child-initiated and we include one such example in the panel.

> *Girl aged 7: We found a coconut*
> *Teacher: Well done! Oh it's an acorn, if we planted it what do you think would*
> *grow?*
> *Girl aged 3: A flower*
> *Teacher: Not quite, if it came off that tree what would grow?*
> *Child: Don't know!*
> *Teacher: OK, let's get a pot, some stones and soil and plant it to see. (With a group of five children) Which way up do you think? I think on its side it will have the most chance. What do you think it will grow into? [Using opportunity presented by children to model growth/wonder and to investigate gives children an investment in it.]*
> *Child: A tree*
> *Teacher: Mmmm, I wonder what kind?*
> (Document 106 NC obs 6)

Promoting good interactions

Lack of resources should not be a barrier to promoting good adult-child interactions: staff themselves are the main resource in any communication-friendly setting. Practitioners who respond to and value all of children's attempts at communication support them with language appropriate to individual development in one-to-one and in group sessions. They encourage talk, use sensitive observation to interpret needs and reflect these in language. They support children in both free play and group times and use positive language with and in front of children. They encourage children to share books with each other and ensure that children have opportunities to speak in their own language if English is not their first language. The revised framework makes clear that children should be given opportunities to learn and reach a good standard in English during the EYFS. When children do not have skills in English, practitioners must explore the child's skills in the home language with parents to identify any language delays.

Promoting interactions with children requires adults to think carefully before asking questions to give children time to respond. In settings where this takes place it is often the case that displays are used interactively to encourage talk. These are intended to stimulate discussion because practitioners know that children who are curious and interested will ask questions. Resources too will be at child height, labelled with symbols or pictures and words in the languages of the setting. Quiet areas for storytelling and reading together are offered with soft cushions and furnishings which convey that this is an area to sit and share stories. The provision of quiet areas for reflection and thinking and quiet conversations outside is essential. Practitioners introduce new vocabulary in their planning and ensure there are opportunities for adults to use new words regularly so they become part of children's repertoire. There are opportunities to read and reread favourite books. Times to sing and say rhymes take place regularly with children as a planned group activity or when they spontaneously occur and stories and songs come alive with props or puppets and supported by physical actions.[16]

Interaction between children and adults '*is not a static process, but a dynamic and fluid activity which is dependent upon the context and the child's needs. There is not one way of interaction but many.*'[17]

Supporting children's interactions requires well-developed communication on the part of the adult. Through observation they come to understand young children's body language and non-verbal communication, when a baby wriggles with excitement or stiffens the whole body when annoyed. Adults can converse with babies before they have developed speech, using a variety of language in their own speech, varying tone and level and pitch, regularly saying finger and action rhymes, nursery rhymes and songs. Other skills will involve telling stories about their lives and the events in them, listening to and encouraging children to do the same; encouraging children to talk about their emotions (especially

boys) and analysing the components of speech and language and progressing these with children.

When sharing books effective practitioners use language that excites and inspires young imaginations. In the book *Proust and the Squid*,[18] the author includes this beautiful reminder to us of the potency of language, '*Children who begin kindergarten having heard and used thousands of words, whose meanings are already understood, classified, and stored away in their young brains, have the advantage on the playing field of education. Children who never have a story read to them, who never hear words that rhyme, who never imagine fighting with dragons or marrying a prince, have the odds overwhelmingly against them*'.

We propose the following strategies to promote quality interactions with children:

Adult interaction strategy	Practical example
Tune in to the child	Listen.
	Observe body language
	Show genuine interest
Clarify what is said	'So what you are saying is ...'
Invite elaboration	'What does this mean exactly?'
Suggest alternatives	'Is there another way to do this?'
Speculate	'Could the story finish differently?'
Repeat and extend	'Bear. Yes, it's a large fierce brown bear, like the one you have at home'
Use open-ended questions	'Why do you think? What if ...?'
Extend thinking	' How do you know?' ' Can you tell me why you think that happened?'

The adult role within communication and language in the EYFS

One of the three characteristics of effective learning in the revised EYFS is 'creating and thinking critically (which we examine in more detail in Chapter 10). Adults support children's thinking through the interactions they have with them in the many conversations throughout the day. In settings this is by joining in with small group interactions and supporting the development of individual language for thinking. Babies' and young children's experiences of the world and their language are limited and therefore the role of the adult is to draw their thinking out and extend it. Sustained shared thinking takes place when adults are aware of a child's interests and understanding and both develop an idea or skill together. In settings and class-rooms, we should aim to create a 'climate for thinking' in which talk is prevalent and where conversations abound. In such a climate, children use language as a tool for thinking and action. They take risks with language and use vocabulary because they feel secure and they know that what they say is valued.

Successful adult interactions extend children's thinking and foster independent thinking by modelling language in their own speech, in giving instructions, in explaining, questioning, praising, introducing new vocabulary, and in conversations with others. Practitioners plan flexibly for it and respond to naturally occurring situations. Many opportunities for thinking emerge from children's own ideas and their engagement with activities both indoors and outdoors where the skilled practitioner encourages talk and children's own ideas. At other times it can be to challenge ideas. Interactions arise from child to child; child to adult and adult to adult. Effective adult-child interactions are based on warm, trusting relationships which encourage positive attitudes to learning. As adults we must enter the child's world, recognize their interests and concerns and have conversations which encourage further thinking. We should seek out opportunities to be involved in, to initiate or respond to conversations but not to direct them: it is often better to wait and be attentive to the child's signals. Having patience leads the adult to join in with the child at his or her level of conversation. Taking the lead from the child and staying with the child's conversation topic affirms the child's feelings of self-worth. Children's own questions and own experiences are excellent starting points for discussions as are the many opportunities that present throughout each day to make thinking visible and to embed thinking in children's own culture, language and learning.

Section review: Communication and language

Thinking

Before the age of five children acquire a vocabulary of about 10,000 words.[19]

How can a baby room be organised to allow for individual attention and conversation?

How is this different to the language environment for a two year old?

What does a language-rich environment for four to five year olds look like?

Reflecting

Look at the Communication and Language section of the revised Development Matters document (pages 15–21). Concentrate on the column headed Positive

Relationships/What adults could do. Think about your own practice as you read the examples of good practice for each development stage.

Doing

Work with a small group of children. Set up an activity and record the conversations that take place. Then play it back afterwards and analyse it. Now consider these questions:

Who does the most talking and what types of talk can you hear?

What messages does this give the children?

What are the implications for your practice?

Conclusion

Early relationships with a caring adult help a child develop secure attachments. Initially this is with a parent or carer and later in settings with the child's key person, providing an ideal base for a child to set out and explore the world confidently. This sound foundation builds stability, curiosity, persistence and independence all of which are fundamental for the development of relationships building, success in school and for lifelong learning. Language allows the expression of emotions. The keys to connecting language, thinking and learning are warm and positive interactions.

9 Parents, Partnerships and Home Learning Matters

Aims of the chapter

- To discuss the significant role that parents and families play in children's lives in supporting their development and learning throughout the EYFS
- To explore issues in partnership working with parents and carers
- To explore research findings which highlight the powerful influence of the home learning environment for children from birth to five years of age
- To identify best practice in home-school/setting partnerships

This chapter begins by emphasising the importance of working in partnership with parents: an important message that permeates the revised EYFS framework. We put forward the case that parenting is a key factor in determining children's life chances then discuss what working together with parents and families in the early years means. We welcome that this partnership is high on the government agenda but raise some issues and challenges that emerge from new government policy. We then consider partnerships with parents and carers and present a number of short vignettes that provide excellent real-life examples of this work in practice. Finally, we present research evidence that home learning partnerships matter not only in the short-term, but that they influence later outcomes as children continue their journeys through primary school and beyond. We provide a number of practical suggestions to consider ways that work with parents can impact the home learning environment for children.

Working together with parents and families in the early years

The Introduction to the revised EYFS states that *good parenting and high quality early learning together provide the foundation children need to make the most of their abilities and talents as they grow up*.[1] The benefits of parental involvement in children's learning have been known since the influential Plowden[2] report of the 1960s. Children's life trajectories are significantly influenced by what happens to them in the early years and the experiences in the home environment and the parenting they receive have a direct and long-lasting impact on their life chances. The learning environment provided by parents begins even before a child is born and since almost three-quarters of a young child's life is spent with the family and wider community, the home becomes the significant learning environment.

Early years professionals have always placed high value on meaningful partnerships with parents and families. In her review of the EYFS Dame Clare Tickell[3] reminded us, *where parents and carers are actively encouraged to participate confidently in their children's learning and healthy development, the outcomes for children will be at their best.* This approach is threaded throughout the new framework. At the heart of partnership working is the child, whose rights and entitlements are fundamental for all work with children. Article 3 of the UN Convention on the Rights of the Child tells us that the best interests of children should always be a priority. This, according to the Early Childhood Forum should be the core principle of all partnership arrangements, indicating that working with families is a journey of trust where strong, respectful relationships are required. This implies sharing not only information, but responsibility and accountability. Mutual respect and a genuine value of each other are central to partnership working. This of course requires a position where both partners have equal status and are joint stakeholders committed to the benefit of the child. Practitioners can learn from parents just as parents can learn from the expertise of well qualified and well informed practitioners. It is a joint responsibility. Being a parent in the current climate brings considerable challenges and many parents welcome support from settings and from wider services in response to changing circumstances, such as when a child's development is causing concern.

Parent partnership initiatives in the past have had proven successes. The Parents Early Years and Learning (PEAL) project, begun in 2005, reported improved engagement of parents with settings; increased parental knowledge and confidence and better engagement in children's learning.

Another example, the Peers Early Education Partnership project (PEEP), an intervention aimed at adults working with children under five in disadvantaged communities reported positive effects on literacy and numeracy levels and self-esteem.[4] Family learning programmes aimed at developing adult literacy and numeracy and supporting children's learning have had a considerable success for both children and adults. In an Ofsted survey[5] among almost all of the providers surveyed, adults were developing good or very good skills, behaviours and parenting attitudes or were achieving success in gaining qualifications. The contributions of parent support advisers, family and health workers, mentors and teachers to family learning sessions were invaluable. These and many other local initiatives support the continued funding of early years provision with parental partnerships. The social and economic benefits of early intervention are strongly expressed in Graham Allen's review[6] *Early Intervention: The Next Steps* and consistently demonstrated good returns on this investment. Despite this confirmation, the report found that that major investment in the previous ten years had not paid the dividends expected: an important point for the current government to heed in policy-making and allocation of funding with respect to the early years.

Supporting parents in their role

The vital contribution of parents and families was brought to the foreground in the *Children's Plan* (2007) produced under the last Labour Government. The coalition government's vision for families in the early years is to support all new parents as they make the transition to parenthood, through pregnancy and then in the important first few months after birth. It considers it imperative that parents feel supported in their role and that parents' skills are developed to fully support their children' s development and learning. There is a recognition of the need for advice and guidance in this area – mainly provided through health visitor support and information provided online through the Foundation Years website.[7]

The care and nurturance that parents and other adults provide for young children has a lasting effect on their health and development. Throughout history, grandparents too have been partners in children's care and learning and indeed some grandparents are primary caregivers for their grandchildren, while for others, the involvement may be temporary. They provide experience and life perspective and alongside parents, grandparents are important influences and a resource for today's families. The Families and Early Years Analysis and Research Team at the DFE requested a brief review[8] of research evidence and statistical data on grandparents providing childcare in England. It found that:

- Grandparents played a prominent role in providing child care and supporting maternal employment, especially for low income families.
- Grandparents were the main child care arrangement for 35% of families where

the mother was working or studying when the child was nine months old, ahead of all other types of care.

- Grandparents continued to have a significant role in child care arrangements when children started school, particularly during holiday periods.
- There was some evidence that children receiving informal childcare (primarily grandparents) in their first few years of life had as good or better vocabularies but did less well on numeracy and literacy tests; were more likely to be overweight; had higher levels of hyperactivity and peer difficulties. In some cases the relationship only held for children from more advantaged homes.

Parenting skills and parent-child relationships determine children's well-being and to a large degree their subsequent life chances. The DfE is leading a national parenting campaign to raise awareness of the importance of high-quality parenting skills,[9] of building good family relationships for children in the foundation years and promoting practice-informed evidence that supports parental engagement in their children's learning. So strong is the government's view of the value of positive parenting, that in October 2011 the Minister of State for Children and Families, Sarah Teather announced a two year trial of universal parenting classes for parents of children aged up to five in three local areas: Middlesbrough, the London Borough of Camden and Derbyshire. The DFE website for that date announced this free trial was being offered to over 50,000 mothers and fathers and claimed that three-quarters of parents surveyed wanted information and help with parenting. The proposed content of the classes includes:

- how to promote positive behaviour with better communication and listening skills
- managing conflict
- the importance of mothers and fathers working as a team
- the appropriate play for age/development
- understanding the importance of boundaries and routines to children
- firm, fair and consistent approaches to discipline
- strengthening positive relationships in the family.

These initiatives and the practical impact they have on parents and children in the EYFS have not yet been evaluated.

Section review: Working together with parents and families in the early years

Thinking

Parenting is deemed to be the hardest job in the world but are parenting programmes the answer to giving parents the necessary skills? Is there a danger that such programmes might undermine parents' confidence, rather than boost it by making parenting into yet another course that is taught by specialists?

Reflecting

Reflect on your own practice.

- Do parents understand the setting's policies on areas such as learning and teaching, inclusion and behaviour?
- Does the documentation provided for parents in your setting value parental involvement and their role in children's learning and development?
- Do parents regularly review their child's progress with you? Do parents contribute to children's learning journeys?
- Do all staff listen to and value what parents say?
- Are workshops and other sessions provided to involve parents and extend their learning?

Doing

Undertake a short survey with parents in your setting or school. You could discuss the following issues with parents/carers:

- What is important for your children?
- How do you feel about the drive in early years for children to achieve in school? How do you feel about the importance of emotional, social and emotional capabilities (e.g. empathy, self-regulation)?
- Do you think these are as important as more traditional measures of literacy, numeracy and academic qualifications? Do you see a relationship between the two?

Consider what is said and how your setting can support parents to understand the relationship between the two.

Partnerships with settings and schools

Scotland's new curriculum framework for children and young people aged three to 18 Building the Curriculum[10] provides good advice in relation to working in partnership with parents and recommends the following approaches:

- ensure a welcoming and warm environment for all children and their families
- ensure joint approaches to planning, assessing and recording support parents in establishing a sense of ownership of the service
- build capacity, perhaps by offering classes and activities for parents, ensuring that information from parents is genuinely valued and taken into account
- develop effective communication systems
- develop links between the home and setting to ensure consistency of care for babies and young children
- create dedicated space for parents to meet with one another
- consult with parents as part of the self-evaluation process
- ensure parents are an integral part of transition processes.

In England and Wales, as in Scotland, the most successful settings, that is to say those with the best outcomes for children, work in close partnership with parents. There is mutual respect and trust. These settings listen to parents. Mission statements and educational aims are shared with parents. They work hard to understand the families and parents of the children who attend the setting. This knowledge is valued and used by practitioners to inform planning and assessment. There is open communication and on-going dialogue where the views expressed are respected by all partners. There is a common language, which is free from jargon. Written reports and newsletters are clear, take account of literacy levels where appropriate and are accessible to both mothers and fathers. Staff consider alternative ways of engaging families who are more advantaged, for example through electronic communications and accessing and contributing to children's learning journeys on-line. Events are

scheduled at convenient times so that parents who work can attend, an important consideration since one parent working full-time and the other working part-time is a common family arrangement in the UK currently.[11] Many settings already undertake home visits, which provide an opportunity for parents to meet practitioners in a familiar environment and promote opportunities for information sharing and collective decision-making.

Guidance to schools is very similar to that offered to early years settings. Here also the most effective partnerships exist when parents and carers are welcomed and valued participants in their children's learning. Schools with successful partnerships with parents make use of technology to communicate with them, using email, text and phone messages to keep in contact. The use electronic newsletters to keep parents up to date with school news and school websites, along with portals and learning platforms give valuable and instant information to help parents support their child's learning. Initiatives such as Bookstart, Book Time and Booked Up have improved parental engagement in their children's early reading. Other schemes such as Parent Know How, and Parent Support have improved parents' access to information. Schools use a number of practical strategies to successfully engage parents in their children's learning. Examples of good practice from the DCSF[12] are set out below:

- One school produced parent information sheets in a magazine format with photographs of pupils and events, top tips and a visually recognisable, vibrant house style.
- To support literacy and numeracy, a school ran literacy and numeracy workshops for reception parents and carers during the last 30 minutes of the school day. Teachers made a special effort to involve parents who were harder to reach by phone calls, direct contact in the playground and further reminders by phone the day before each workshop. After the first few weeks, the children's enthusiasm to work with their parent or carer secured continued engagement.
- Another school targeted parents and carers of children who were not making expected progress in the reception class and invited them to a short meeting with the teacher. The teacher shared the child's specific curricular targets and modelled activities and games that could be worked on at home. In another school, curricular targets were shared at parents' evenings with pupils in attendance. Parents and carers were encouraged to regularly ask the child about progress towards meeting the targets. Targets were worked on in class,

particularly at the start of the day when parents were invited to spend a few minutes in the classroom with their child doing 'early work'.

- A school set up a parents' forum group which met twice a term. Initially specific parents were invited to join the forum to ensure that the school population was fully represented. The forum was used to shape many aspects of parental engagement and involvement in the school. For example, curriculum information evenings were redesigned to include hands-on workshops and address key areas of learning and the ways in which parents could support learning at home.

Another useful source of practical information[13] presents successful schemes in schools and local authority settings, highlighting different ways to engage parents in their children's learning – from schemes concentrating on attainment to others where social and emotional needs are prioritised. What is demonstrated is that 'at home' learning is helped when formal learning in classrooms and more informal learning at home are brought together. Examples of how this can happen are given below:

Home-school influences	School-home influences
<ul><li>engaging families in designing activities</li><li>drawing on interests and home culture</li><li>making use of resources and artefacts from the home</li><li>parents discussing and sharing experiences of supporting their children's learning at home</li></ul>	<ul><li>opportunities for parents to meet with a cross-section of school staff</li><li>introducing themes or concepts from the school curriculum</li><li>engaging parents in learning both for themselves and with their children</li><li>showcasing or explaining teaching methods</li></ul>

Other practical strategies for effective partnerships working through home-school/setting links include:

- modelling positive parent-child interactions, such as through the use of play or reading routines that can be adapted to the home learning environment
- giving formative feedback to reinforce the learning outcomes achieved by parents and their children

- building on family interests and home culture
- empowering parents in the design of 'take home' games or activities to extend the influence of the schemes and to engage wider family members
- providing written records and/or organising events to celebrate the families' achievements and to disseminate the schemes to other parents and pupils.[14]

Section review: Partnerships with settings and schools

Thinking

Children's learning is greatly helped when more formal learning in settings and classrooms is brought together with informal learning that goes on at home. Are there barriers for this to happen? What opportunities does this provide? How can we reach and support parents who are reluctant to be involved?

Reflecting

The Ofsted website Parent View[15] has seen more than 14,000 parents responding to the online questionnaire with concerns about bullying, behaviour and homework. Are these issues a concern in the early years and if so what is your school or setting doing to address such issues and work more closely with parents?

Doing

Early years settings have always valued the unique contributions made by parents and families. Review your policy for partnership working with parents to ensure it reflects the value placed by the school or setting on parents as partners in their children's learning. A written policy is important to:

- Show how its work with parents is a key feature of the setting/school's overall policy and approach.
- Make clear what is expected of everyone and what can be achieved.
- Spell out the links between clear principles and effective action.
- Provide points of reference for consistency of practice.
- Support the induction of new teachers/practitioners.
- Encourage development by providing a framework for regularly reviewing progress and achievement.
- Form the basis for planning a whole-school/setting approach.

Does your current policy reflect the above?

Home learning

The Centre Forum, representing the views of the Liberal party, indicated recently that *'the single most important factor influencing a child's intellectual and social development is the quality of parenting and care they receive and the quality of the Home Learning Environment that this creates'*.[16] Research supports the importance of the home learning environment (HLE) and confirms that a child's experiences at home have life-long consequences on learning and developmental outcomes. As it has been demonstrated: *'Parents' involvement in children's activities and the beliefs and aspirations they hold, along with a stimulating home environment have been identified as having a significant effect on children's levels of educational achievement'*.[17] Researchers found that *'at home good parenting'* has a greater effect on children's achievement than other factors and means a secure and stable environment, where intellectual stimulation takes place and there are high aspirations for the child.[18]

What parents do at home with their children is far more important than their own social class or academic qualifications. The home environment has a greater influence on children's achievement than inherited ability or the quality of pre-school and school provision.[19] Another review[20] highlighted the importance of the HLE in supporting language and literacy development as well as the development of mathematical language. The effect of early home learning on outcomes at age five was also found to have a greater effect than parental background factors of socio-economic status, mother's qualifications and family income.[21]

We interpret the term 'home learning' as wider than merely the activities a child does at home. We see it as the range of experiences that provide the foundation from which children can grow to fulfil their full potential.

When the right experiences are provided at home they make a real difference to children's lives. They are instrumental in narrowing the gap between children from different social backgrounds.[22] Children's experiences in the early years have a powerful influence on developing their cognitive abilities.[23] While family factors such as parents' education and socio-economic status are important, the extent of home learning activities exerts a greater and independent influence on children's cognitive development at three years of age.[24] This is the critical period for parents to have the most dramatic effect on a child's learning.

Home learning matters not only in the short-term, but influences later outcomes as children continue their journeys through primary and secondary school and beyond. Parental interest in their child's education has four times more influence on attainment by the age of 16 than socio-economic background.[25] When parents are involved with their children's early learning at home, there are benefits on attainment and social behavior at ages seven and ten.[26] Other studies show that a relationship between family circumstances and children's cognitive development is present well before the age of five.[27] Such evidence indicates that the causes of low academic achievement may lie partly in the experiences during the early years. In other words, low achievement may be in part due to the experiences (or lack of experiences) a child has at home.

Links with parents and carers in the EYFS

What can parents do at home to benefit their children's learning? It should be reassuring to parents that the answers do not require huge financial outlay or time investments or indeed specialist skills to make a difference. The EYFS Parents' Guide[28] is a document purporting to help parents understand the new EYFS framework. It explains that activities at home are important if parents are to support their child's learning and development and have a really long lasting effect on learning through school. We regret that an opportunity was lost here to produce both a more attractive document and give messages that are less simplistic to the whole spectrum of parents.

To build a foundation for learning at home for babies and toddlers we include the following activities to extend learning at home which practitioners may model alongside parents:

Communicate warmly with the baby	Use eye-contact and smiles
Hold and touch the child gently	Listen to and talk with the child
Involve the child in everyday routines such as washing up, sorting washing	Offer stimulating objects to a baby to look at and explore
Play together letting the baby take the lead	Tell stories
	Introduce books

In addition, with older pre-school children the following activities should be encouraged:

Listen to the child	Spend time talking with the child (about everyday events, familiar people, colours, shapes, numbers, letters)
Share books	Sing songs and nursery rhymes
Paint and draw. Encourage mark-making	Investigate numbers and shapes in real everyday contexts

Play with letters and numbers	Visit the library. Visits parks and do this in different seasons.
Introduce the alphabet	Bake together. Plant seeds.
Take the child on visits	Create regular opportunities to play with friends

Encourage an interest in letters and the sounds of words

The Five R's below, developed by a school in Hertfordshire, can help parents to be aware of the conditions that will support children's learning – these are distributed to parents in some schools[29] and could be displayed in settings or classrooms:

1 *Ready to learn.* Provide a secure home environment. Build relationships with your child that foster confidence. Promote a desire to learn and a willingness to learn.
2 *Resourceful.* Use things that are already in the home. Being resourceful is about encouraging children to use everyday things to play with and learn from.
3 *Resilient.* Encourage your child to stick at something and not give up. Use encouragement to keep children trying even when mistakes are made.
4 *Remembering.* Have fun practising and repeating different games and activities that build memory and concentration skills.
5 *Reflective.* Look back at what your child has achieved. Help your child think about how h/she did this. Let him or her copy what you do; experiment; help your child learn by experience. Provide support and reassurance; give praise and encouragement.

Conclusion

We know that what happens in the first years of a child's life is crucial in helping each child grow into a well-functioning individual. There is considerable evidence that families and parents have a vital role to play in this. Stable and loving relationships in families are vital for children's progress and well-being and parents are a child's first and most enduring educators. Their role, as we have argued throughout this chapter, is more significant and has greater effect than any other. Parenting is, however, not without its immediate challenges and many parents are in need of additional support in fulfilling this vital role. Whether the initiatives planned in the coalition government go far enough to realising this on the ground remains to be seen. Initiatives like parenting classes are one way that may provide some of the skills needed for parenting in this period when extended families are rare. When high quality settings and schools work closely with parents and carers there are clear benefits for very young children. We have presented some examples of partnership working with parents and some practical ways to achieve this with parents through considering ways to support the home learning environment for children in the Early Years.

Learning and Pedagogy

10

Aims of the chapter

- To identify how children learn and how learning is constructed in the EYFS
- To explore the three characteristics of effective teaching and learning in the EYFS: playing and exploring; active learning; creating and thinking critically
- To explore pedagogy and consider the relationship between teaching and learning throughout the EYFS

We begin this chapter by discussing how learning takes place even before birth. In the first section we look at learning in the womb and trace the beginning of a child's learning journey showing that even before they are born, babies and young children have the capacity to learn and remember. Next we turn attention to the three characteristics of effective learning in the revised EYFS: playing and exploring; active learning and creating and thinking critically. We expand on these with reference to the accompanying Development Matters[1] and give examples of these in practice. The chapter finishes by discussing the pedagogy that best supports children's learning and proposes our own core pedagogical principles to implement the EYFS effectively.

Learning begins before birth

A foetus begins learning in the womb through its developing senses. Touch is the first sense to develop at around eight weeks, and through their collisions with the walls of the mother's womb babies begin to learn about the experience of touch and of pain. They learn about taste and smell as early as six months through the amniotic fluid they swallow from what the mother eats. From about four months when their eyes start to open, they are learning about the dark environment of the womb. Information about this is transmitted through the optic nerves in the eyes to the occipital cortex in the brain. Babies learn about the position of their body in the womb through the sense of proprioception, which tells them when they are upright, when they are upside down, and helps them to turn around in the womb. A foetus responds to the sound of the mother's heartbeat and even some loud noises in the external environment. Even before children are born, they have the capacity to learn and remember information.

Early experiences help to build babies' growing brains, foster their language skills and nurture positive attitudes to learning. A newborn's brain is built for learning. Weighing in at around 1500 grams, it is more powerful than any desktop computer. It will allow a child to speak a language, to read, to move around and use tools such as paint brushes, scissors or gardening tools with considerable skill, respond emotionally to situations and engage in play with other children. The foundations for learning are laid in the womb and after a child is born, learning continues to accelerate. Newborn babies are eager to learn, and they are geared to move. Growth in the cerebellum area of the brain helps them to integrate sensory information to guide movement. They will quickly learn about the strange new world and to communicate with those around them. Although not yet able to speak and having what appears little control over their arms and legs, a baby is all the time trying to understand what his or her body can do and making sense of everything that is going on. This baby is an active explorer and learner.

There is now considerable evidence[2] that babies think, reason and build mental models of the world, which are refined through their experiences and it is here that the practitioner's role is crucial. Experience alters the architecture of the brain, and the richer the experiences a child has, the more brain development is enhanced and the more powerful the child's learning capacities. At about one third of adult weight at birth, a child's brain matures at an astonishing rate. By the time a child is one year old brain size is 70% that of an adult. A year later, it is 80% adult size. By age three it will be three quarters of full adult weight and a phenomenal learning machine.

The process of learning

Children's learning is affected by many factors so let us now explore the process of learning in more detail with reference to some key ideas and theories. You will see that this discussion on children's learning also includes the important role of the adult. This is, as Pascal and Bertram note,[3] because of the symbiotic relationship that exists between the child and the adult and we expand on this in the section on pedagogy later in this chapter.

Learning may be thought of as the process that brings together intellectual, emotional and environmental influences to enhance existing skills or knowledge, and learning theories describe how this process takes place. Among traditional learning theories such as behaviourism, cognitivism and constructivism, it was constructivism and the work of Piaget and Bruner that revolutionised learning in schools and settings and whose legacy is still evident today. This approach sees children constructing their own meaning from the experiences they have. The role of the adult is as a facilitator who provides contexts for learning that encourage children to solve problems and construct meaning for themselves.

Critics of Piaget refute his notion of fixed stages,[4] but later research confirms that children at the pre-operational stage, from two to seven years in Piaget's stages, do understand number conversation and they do have a developing theory of mind that allows them to understand and predict the thinking of others. Recent research argues that cognitive skills can be altered by experience and training. For example, as children mature they use better encoding, strategy construction, automatisation and generalisation techniques to make sense of the experiences they have had as learning mechanisms.[5] Another theory[6] proposes that changes in children's thinking, and therefore their ability to learn, result from changes to information processing capacity or 'm space' which indicates that learning is affected by how well children use their limited memory capacity.

Let us illustrate this with an example from the EYFS: a four year old is engaged in a mathematical activity with a practitioner. A child of this age might be able to count out six sweets in groups of two in a line by counting one sweet at a time. Whereas older children in Key Stage 1, whose memory space is larger and whose processing speed is greater, will use strategies like grouping to solve the problem more quickly.

We know, in addition, that there are cultural and social dimensions to learning which Piaget's theories downplayed. Learning does not take place in a social vacuum, but alongside other people and events. Children's constructions of reality and meaning are based as much on the understandings of others as they are on their own constructions. For young children, most of what they learn is through the interactions they have with others, and not through deliberate attempts at instruction. Vygotsky[7] placed emphasis on the child's interactions with 'significant others' such as teachers, parents and peers. It is through these verbal and written interactions that children internalize the skills and values that are important in their society and thus develop their thinking. He saw the importance of knowing a child's actual developmental level (i.e. what they know and can do *now*) and then moving them to the next level with intervention from an adult or more able peer. The distance between the two levels is known as the 'zone of proximal development' (ZPD).

Learning and the EYFS

The EYFS seeks to provide a secure foundation through learning and development opportunities planned around the needs and interests of every child. Practitioners should therefore plan learning experiences for children in the ZPD so they can explore what children know now and how they can be helped to extend their learning to the next level.

Information-processing theories explain learning by exploring brain processes that act on information in the environment. The difference in the way that adults and children think and solve problems has emerged as 'fuzzy trace theory'.[8] This proposes that children under the age of six use verbatim representations in their encoding, while older children use fuzzy representations. This accounts for the slower speed at which younger children encode information: they become immersed in the detail which interferes with the use of other strategies to solve the problem.

Neuroscience has emerged as a field of learning that many educators have seized upon because it connects brain processes and memory with classroom learning experiences.[9] Brain-based learning theories view learning not as organized centrally but as component parts that work together, with perhaps as many as 70 or more components involved. Neurons join through the synapses between them resulting in learning and this may explain sensitive periods since neural circuits mature at different rates. As outlined briefly in previous chapters, there are many sensitive periods in our lives, each corresponding to a particular brain function and these are most frequent in young children as the brain is undergoing enormous structural changes. First-hand experiences provided by quality environments and interactions at home and in settings modify and support further synaptic connections while unnecessary ones are pruned.[10]

Cognitive skills used in learning such as focused attention, memory and concentration require the active involvement of the learner. Involvement is central to the work on experiential learning by Ferre Laevers.[11] Picture a child totally engaged in an activity such as painting for example: thinking and doing at the limit of her capability and seemingly quite oblivious to everything else that is going on around her. The flow of energy is almost palpable. There is no space between the child and the activity, just absorption, her total focus of attention is in the activity and the pleasure of engaging.

Creativity is fundamental to successful learning. In a recent Ofsted survey of primary schools[12] which included two nursery schools, inspectors found evidence of improved standards and strong personal development when pupils were encouraged to:

- develop their understanding by questioning what had been presented to them
- imagine what might be
- make connections and present their ideas to their peers for review.

These schools had aspirations for pupils to ask questions independently, make connections between ideas, think creatively, challenge and participate effectively and reflect on their learning.

Children in the EYFS learn best from real-life experiences, such as cooking real food and using real tools. In the best settings learning is authentic. Practitioners help children relate new knowledge to what they know already and build up schemas or organized ways of making sense of their experiences. With babies, early schemas are created through sensorimotor perceptions (e.g. sucking or banging a rattle provides information about that object for the child). As the child matures, thinking becomes more internalized. At this stage the work of Chris Athey[13] is extremely helpful in advancing our knowledge of schema formation and the 'forms of thought' of young children. Learning requires time; time to practise a skill for example. Observe a toddler learning to walk: this milestone event does not happen successfully on the first attempt. There are many attempts needed before the skill is learned. For learning to take place, children must be inclined to want to learn, and they need to have the dispositions to learn. Dispositions cover attitudes to learning, the will, desire and habits of mind to learn. They also include respect for others, being open to consider alternatives, showing readiness to listen to others. These are affected by the child's personality, the support of family, culture and attitudes to learning that begin at an early age.

Margaret Carr[14] has written extensively on these areas which are central to the New Zealand early years curriculum 'Te Whariki'. She describes five learning dispositions:

- taking an interest
- being involved

- persisting with difficulty
- communicating with others
- taking responsibility.

Guy Claxton's work on learning dispositions[15] adds to our knowledge here. He proposes 17 dispositions or learning capacities which he groups into four groups:

- Resilience, the emotional and attentional aspects of learning such as perseverance, absorption and concentration.
- Resourcefulness which refers to the cognitive aspects of learning like asking questions and making connections.
- Reciprocity is the social dimension of learning and includes collaboration and being receptive to others.
- Reflection which includes planning processes, application and metalearning.

In order to learn, children need to be motivated, and the importance of motivation in the learning process is reflected in the words of renowned social and developmental psychologist, Professor Carol Dweck: '*motivation is the most important factor in determining whether you succeed in the long run. What I mean by motivation is not only the desire to achieve, but also the love of learning, the love of challenge and the ability to thrive on obstacles*'.[16] Motivation takes two forms: intrinsic motivation where the child takes part in the activity without the need for praise or reward for the value of the activity itself, and extrinsic motivation where rewards such as praise, stars or merit points are given, usually by adults.

The child sitting alone engrossed in doing a puzzle at a table is showing intrinsic motivation. The same child appreciates that effort is needed to complete the puzzle and is willing to give this to finish it. For children to be good learners, they need to have a 'growth mindset', not a 'fixed mindset'. We see the latter in children who will only try things they know they will be successful at (e.g. tasting a new food, reaching up high on the climbing frame, etc). Instead we should aim to develop a growth mindset in our children, characterized by learners who are excited by challenge, enjoy learning new things and putting their knowledge and skills to use.

How learning is described and promoted in the revised EYFS

In the Literature Review[17] that informed the new EYFS framework, children's learning is succinctly described as arising from the *'inter-connected and dynamic facets of the unique child with surrounding relationships and experiences'*. This model underpins the revised areas of learning in the new framework and is the rationale behind the three prime and four specific areas. Children interact with their environment, communicating with others and by engaging physically in the experiences and opportunities it offers them. These are universal to all cultures.

The prime areas of Personal, Social and Emotional Development, Communication and Language and Physical Development are at the centre of all learning and development and influence later success in life. As we described earlier, the areas are inter-connected. Personal, Social and Emotional Development for example is connected to Physical Development since a child who is confident will be more willing to explore his or her surroundings. It is connected to Communication and Language through sharing and communicating with others. Similarly, Communication and Language supports Personal, Social and Emotional Development since a child who does communicate with others develops a strong sense of self. There are opportunities for adults to develop Physical Development by talking to children about what it means to be healthy. Physical Development supports Personal, Social and Emotional Development through increased confidence and supports Communication and Language through children talking to others about their movement and physical actions.

The EYFS framework highlights key characteristics of learning for young children. These are the essential features which help children to be effective learners and which underpin the seven areas of learning. The three identified characteristics of effective learning are:

1 Playing and exploring
   - Finding out and exploring
   - Using what they know in their play
   - Being willing to have a go
2 Active learning
   - Being involved and concentrating
   - Keeping on trying
   - Enjoying achieving what they set out to do

3 Creating and thinking critically
   – Having their own ideas
   – Using what they already know to learn new things
   – Choosing ways to do things and finding new ways

The Development Matters[18] document gives guidance on each of the three characteristics.

Playing and exploring

This characteristic is all about engagement. To illustrate this let us turn to the descriptions in A Unique Child/Observing how a child is learning:

Finding out and exploring

- Showing curiosity about objects, events and people
- Using senses to explore the world around them
- Engaging in open-ended activity
- Showing particular interests

Playing with what they know

- Pretending objects are things from their experience
- Representing their experiences in play
- Taking on a role in their play
- Acting out experiences with other people

Being willing to 'have a go'

- Initiating activities
- Seeking challenge
- Showing a 'can do' attitude
- Taking a risk, engaging in new experiences, and learning by trial and error

To explore how you could support the child, use the column Positive Relationships/What adults could do.

Examples include:

- Encourage (children) to explore, and show you own interest in discovering new things.
- Model pretending an object is something else.
- Develop roles and stories.
- Encourage children to try new activities and to judge risks for themselves.
- Talk about how you and the children get better at things through effort and practice and what can be leaned when things go wrong.

The final column on the page, Enabling Environments/What adults could provide gives further support.

Examples include:

- Provide stimulating resources which are accessible and open-ended so they can be used, moved and combined in a variety of ways.
- Plan first-hand experiences and challenges appropriate to the development of the child.
- Arrange flexible indoor and outdoor space and resources where children can explore, build, move and role-play.

In Chapter 7 of this book we set out a strong rationale for the role of play and discussed the connection between play and learning. It is *'what children and young people do in their own time, for their own reasons. When playing, children choose what to do, how to do it and who to do it with. Play takes many forms: doing nothing in particular; doing lots; being boisterous; showing off; being contemplative; being alone; being social; being challenged; being thwarted; overcoming difficulties. Through play, children explore the world and learn to take responsibility for their own choices'.*[19] These words reflect the meaning of playing and learning explored in the revised framework well.

Play provides a context for young children to find out and explore using their senses and their whole bodies to do so. It supports narrative thinking and brings together what they currently know and understand. By providing heuristic play for babies, such as using treasure baskets, we can facilitate mathematical and scientific learning through exploring, sorting, weighing and comparing objects.

In addition play of course is a great facilitator of language and is a powerful context in which to test ideas and solve problems. In her work with nursery children, one writer[20] described the sheer excitement of children learning through discovery play as they experimented with cornflour 'gloop'. She described how the children were learning about materials and their properties as they were encouraged to describe the feel of the materials in their own words and were clearly motivated with this hands-on discovery learning. These children are demonstrating the first characteristic of effective learning, 'finding out and exploring' the properties of the gloop. In this they 'play with what they know', starting from what is familiar to them being keen to test their ideas further and are 'willing to have a go'.

In this example we capture a similar experience of playing and exploring with two three year olds engaging in learning and enjoying finding out about the properties of paint.

The practitioner Anna had set out large rolls of paper on the floor in a corner of the nursery. She began to squirt some yellow paint onto the paper, then some green. Tonia and Khalim were clearly interested and gathered around. 'What is your favourite colour, Tonia?' asked Anna. Tonia replied, 'I like purple'. The children did not know what colours were needed to make purple so they decided to find out. With help from Anna, Tonia squirted some blue paint onto the paper. She gave Khalim some red paint and he did the same. Anna talked about how colours mix together to make a different colour and the children set about finding out what happened when they mixed these colours. They used their hands to rub the paint onto the paper with big sweeping movements; some fast and some slow. They talked about what was happening. They observed when the red and blue paint was mixed together and were delighted as the two colours gradually became one. Tonia's favourite, purple.

Active learning

The second characteristic is active learning which is all about motivation. It has long been accepted that children learn best through active experiences with people, materials, events and ideas rather than through direct teaching or sequenced exercises.[21]

Active learning provides opportunities for children to be independent and make decisions.

- They make choices about the activities they want to engage in and what resources to use.
- They plan and ask questions.
- As they become absorbed in finding out and investigating for themselves, they feel a sense of achievement and their confidence and self-esteem increases.

This is enhanced further when finished articles are valued by adults in the setting. To illustrate this let us turn to the descriptions in A Unique Child/ Observing how a child is learning:

Being involved and concentrating

- Maintaining focus on their activity for a period of time
- Showing high levels of energy, fascination
- Not easily distracted
- Paying attention to details

Keeping on trying

- Persisting with activity when challenges occur
- Showing a belief that more effort or a different approach will pay off
- Bouncing back after difficulties

Enjoying achieving what they set out to do

- Showing satisfaction in meeting their own goals
- Being proud of how they accomplished something – not just the end result
- Enjoying meeting challenges for their own sake rather than external rewards or praise

Now refer to the column Positive Relationships/What adults could do.

Examples include:

- Support children to choose their activities.
- Help children to become aware of their own goals.
- Describe what you see them trying to do and encourage them to talk about their own processes and successes.
- Be specific when you praise.
- Talk about learning rather than just directing.

Further support is given in in Enabling Environments/What adults could provide. Examples are:

- Provide something that is new and unusual for them to explore.
- Notice what arouses children's curiosity, looking for signs of deep involvement to identify learning that is intrinsically motivated.
- Make space and time for all children to contribute.

We illustrate active learning as the second characteristic of effective learning in this scenario.

Reception children Matthew and Simon had been learning about castles. They decided to build a fortress like the ones in pictures they had seen of medieval castles. They planned together the castle they would construct. They decided upon wooden blocks and gathered a large number of blocks together in the construction area. Then they decided it would be better to have a plan on paper so they found a piece of paper and after much discussion drew out what their castle would look like. They then set to work, totally engrossed in the activity for about 30 minutes. During this time other children came over and asked them about their construction, questions which they were able to answer readily. There came a natural pause after this time and the castle was finished. They just needed to design a colourful flag for the top turret. The boys stood back and admired their work. Simon suggested they ask Miss Sampson, the reception teacher help them write a sign about the castle and they ask her if the castle can be kept up until the end of the week. Two proud architects and builders displaying active learning!

Creating and thinking critically

This third characteristic of effective learning is concerned with:

- How children have their own ideas.
- How they generate new ideas, seek out challenges for themselves and explore ways to solve problems.
- The critical creative thinker is organised.
- S/he makes choices, plans and monitors strategies according to the situation encountered.
- S/he makes predictions.
- H/she generates rules in games and link concepts in the quest to discover meaning.
- These thinkers make creative connections in their learning and make maximum use of the opportunities provided for them..
- They use what they already know to learn new things. Often this is not about an end product such as painting a picture and it is certainly not found in a worksheet or the same celebratory card that everyone else is making.
- They use, and are assisted to do this by skilful adults, their experiences in the home and the wider environment to connect their learning.
- There are important messages here about valuing individuality and originality and how professionals value the different types of expressiveness that children demonstrate.

In Development Matters turn to the descriptions in A Unique Child/Observing how a child is learning

Having their own ideas

- Thinking of ideas
- Finding ways to solve problems
- Finding new ways to do things

Making links

- Making links and noticing patterns in their experience
- Making predictions

- Testing their ideas
- Developing ideas of grouping, sequences, cause and effect

Choosing ways to do things

- Planning, making decisions about how to approach a task, solve a problem and reach a goal
- Checking how well their activities are going
- Changing strategy as needed
- Reviewing how well the approach worked

Refer to the column Positive Relationships/What adults could do. Examples here are:

- Model being a thinker, showing that you don't always know, are curious and sometimes puzzled, and can think and find out.
- Encourage open-ended thinking.
- Give children time to think and talk.
- Model the creative process, showing your thinking about some of the many possible ways forward.
- Encourage children to describe problems they encounter and to suggest ways to solve the problem.
- Show and talk about strategies – how to do things – including problem-solving, thinking and learning.
- Give feedback.

Further support is given in Enabling Environments/What adults could provide. Examples are:

- Build in opportunities for children to play with materials before using them in planned tasks.
- Routines can be flexible.
- Plan linked experiences that follow the ideas children are really thinking about.
- Use mind maps.
- Develop a learning community which focuses on how, and not just what we are learning.

In this scenario we move to an outdoor learning environment to see creating and thinking critically in action.

Children in a setting had been learning about heroes. They had recently had a visit from the local fire-brigade who talked to the children about their work and the equipment they used. Afterwards, the children helped build a fire station in the outdoor area and constructed a fire engine from blocks and crates and played with a real hose the fire-brigade had left them. The adult helpers devised an imaginary problem for the children to solve that would use what the group knew about the work of fire-fighters. A fire had started in a nearby building and there had been a call to the local station. How would the children respond? What did they need to do? The scene was quickly transformed. At the station the telephone call was received and details taken down. Three children put on helmets and tunics to respond. Others manned the 'fire-engine' and sped off to the fire. On arrival the hose was unrolled but it was too short. People were trapped. The adults watched as the children came up with ideas and strategies to solve the problem. Eventually it was agreed that two fire-fighters would go and save the people and the remaining fire-fighters would use plastic buckets of water to put the fire out. After a successful rescue, the children and the adults discussed what had happened and the actions they had taken. They wanted the story of the successful rescue to be written down and given to the local sire station and the fire-fighters who had inspired them.

Section review: How learning is constructed in the new EYFS

Thinking

What does being an effective learner mean to you? What does it mean for the children in your setting? Does this correspond with the characteristics of effective learning described in this section?

Reflecting

Why are the three characteristics of effective learning referred to in this chapter important as skills for life as well as important learning skills?

Doing

Plan to try out these strategies to develop children's learning:

- Join in children's play and fit in with their ideas.

- Ensure children have uninterrupted time to play and explore each day.
- Encourage children to learn together and from each other.
- Create time and freedom for children to become deeply involved in activities.
- Value children's questions and avoid rushing to answer them too quickly.
- Plan experiences that link and follow children's own ideas.

Pedagogy matters

In the previous section we presented an image of successful learning when children are curious, investigative, experimental, imaginative, thoughtful and reflective. How can this best be developed and what are the best ways to promote this? John F. Kennedy once said that a child mis-educated is a child lost.

What does the term 'pedagogy' mean? The word is from the Greek to 'lead children to school'. It includes the principles and methods of instruction and the art or science of educating. The word has come to mean both teaching and the ways in which the environment for learning is provided. It does not necessarily mean a didactic transmission of knowledge, but a learning environment with planned opportunities for play and exploration.[22]

The following definition captures its essence neatly:

'*Pedagogy refers to that set of instructional techniques and strategies which enable learning to take place and provide opportunities for the acquisition of knowledge, skills, attitudes and dispositions within a particular social and material context. It refers to the interactive process between teacher and learner and to the learning environment (which includes the concrete learning environment, the family and community).*[23]

Pedagogical models are formed from theories about how children learn and approaches are based on a number of factors, including the specific context of the learning, knowledge of the child, subject or curriculum knowledge, learner motivation, feedback and assessment. The preferred approach for children in the EYFS is a co-constructivist model, which sees the child as an active co-constructor of knowledge; learning actively and experientially. Learning therefore involves both adult and child together. Play is considered a significant way of promoting learning for children in the EYFS since it underpins learning and development.

Pedagogy in the EYFS

The concept of 'playful pedagogy' was introduced earlier and some further expansion of this is appropriate at this point because we propose this as an appropriate approach in the EYFS. A pedagogy of play still remains a work in progress but there is evidence to support the idea of children as 'playful learners'. Academics convening at a Play Research seminar at Leeds Metropolitan University[24] several years ago reported that when children regularly engaged in learning through play, they showed improved performance on problem-solving, number and literacy tasks. Playful learning promotes conflict resolution skills: social and cooperative play have clear links with learning, progression and identity formation. When engaged in playful tasks, which children have initiated, they show higher levels of cognitive self-regulation. There are links between playful meaning-making and the meanings made as children use marks for early writing and for early mathematics – key aspects of children's learning. What then does playful pedagogy look like in supporting children's learning?

When adults have a deep understanding of play and how it is connected to the curriculum children respond at many levels and the inherent potential of playful learning is realized. The revised EYFS provides sufficient flexibility for practitioners to follow children's interests, respond to children's own ideas for developing play activities, and provide structured activities to teach specific knowledge and skills. Playful teaching involves practitioners in knowing when and if to intervene in children's play episodes. Adults can support children's self-initiated play by observing it to develop understanding of the rules of each episode, considering strategies to enter the play and thinking what they, as an invited visitor can offer. It is about being mindful not to lead, but to join in on the child's terms. To be truly tuned in to the child and the flow of the play often  requires the adult to act under the direction of the child, or interact alongside the child, as play partner, fully supporting the play. Adults should observe what is going on and offer suggestions at times but avoid leading the play. Closed questions to satisfy intended learning objectives or assessments should be avoided. The adult should respond flexibly to the child and to the direction the child wishes to take in their play.

Playful teaching does not only happen in child-initiated play. Adult-led activities provide opportunities for introducing new knowledge or ideas and for developing and practising skills. There are times when the activities are prompted by the children and their interests. At other times, adults lead based on their knowledge of individual children and skill in planning learning activities. The activities retain the characteristics of play that are essential for young children's learning. Playful adult-led activities include open-ended opportunities where practitioners observe and support learning and consider next steps or have clear learning objectives matched to children's current knowledge to extend or consolidate what children know and can do. This means:

- presenting tasks in imaginative ways
- ensuring tasks are as open-ended as possible, allowing children to make choices and express their own ideas
- using materials or story-lines that children associate with play
- providing for children's hands-on, active participation.[25]

Informed adults facilitate learning more than resources and equipment and they do this in a number of ways.

- They become involved in children's play when invited to do so.
- They look and listen and they help children make choices.
- They model persistence: for example when a child is distracted and leaves an activity unfinished, this provides an opportunity for the adult to encourage the child to consider the concept of being 'finished' and to directly model perseverance and persistence.
- Adults scaffold learning when 'significant others' help the child at crucial points in the learning and then gradually remove the help as the child becomes successful at the task. Scaffolding is common practice in schools and learning settings where the skilled adult breaks down a task like solving a maths problem and adjusts the help provided as the child proceeds.

The use of open questions is particularly effective here. Try these for example:

- What are you going to do first? Then what?

- What will happen if you …?
- Could you do this another way?
- Is there anything else you need?
- What will it look like when you finish?
- How will you know when you have finished?

In the most effective pedagogy in the EYFS, adults model thinking and appropriate language to children. They encourage sustained shared thinking, which has been defined as *'an episode in which two or more individuals 'work together' in an intellectual way to solve a problem, clarify a concept, evaluate activities, extend a narrative etc. Both parties must contribute to the thinking and it must develop and extend'.*[26]

We see this here where a nursery assistant (NA) and a group of children are working with playdough at a table.

Boy (aged 3:11) hands her a ball of playdough.

NA: 'I wonder what's inside? I'll unwrap it.'

NA quickly makes the ball into a thumb pot and holds it out to the boy.

NA: 'It's empty!'

Boy takes a pinch of playdough and drops it into the thumb pot: 'It's an egg.'

NN picking it out gingerly: 'It's a strange shape.'

[Another child tries to take the 'egg']

NA: 'Be very, very careful. It's an egg.'

To Boy: 'What's it going to hatch into?'

Boy: 'A lion.'

NA: 'A lion?…Oh, I can see why it might hatch into a lion, it's got little hairy bits on it.'

NA sends Boy to put the egg somewhere safe to hatch. He takes the egg and goes into the bathroom.

[After a few minutes, Boy returns to the group.]

NA: 'Has the egg hatched?'

Boy: 'Yes.'

NA: 'What was it?'

Boy: 'A bird.'

NA: 'A bird? We'll have to take it outside at playtime and put it in a tree so it can fly away.'

As you read the example, notice how skilled the practitioner is gently extending the boy's thinking. Her use of questions encourages the boy to think more deeply about the shape of the dough. She refrains from directing or giving the answers and lets the conversation develop to its conclusion. Both practitioner and child are engaged in an episode of sustained shared thinking.

There is often reluctance to use the word 'teaching' in association with young children and yet effective early years pedagogy must still be 'instructive'. Babies and young children should learn informally in ways that are appropriate to their development. Play is the ideal vehicle for this, along with other ways of learning described in the first section in this chapter and in previous chapters. More structured learning should be introduced gradually so that by the end of the reception year, children will learn through a mix of play and small teaching groups, and both child-initiated and adult-led activities will continue to be in evidence. The pedagogic approaches must be fit for purpose; linked to learning outcomes and taking into account context and organization of the children.

Effective pedagogy uses technology to enhance learning. There should be some direct instruction, for example learning the sounds and letters of the alphabet, but there should also be much talk and interaction in pairs and in small groups, where there is time for children to internally rehearse their own ideas and develop skills. They should play and discover for themselves and there should be adult guidance through questioning, modelling and scaffolding. Effective pedagogy in the EYFS follows children's interests. It responds to their ideas for play activities and develops them. It provides structured activities through creative and playful adult-guided activities that teach specific knowledge and skills.

An example of this in practice concerns Ali aged four years.
Ali attends a private day nursery and has recently returned from Bangladesh. His family speak Bengali at home and Ali rarely speaks English at the nursery. His key person, Satti knows how much he likes toy cars and joins him pushing two small vehicles on the carpet. She watches him at play for several minutes before initiating a conversation in Bengali.

Satti: 'Hi Ali. I see you like cars.'
Ali nods.
Satti: 'Great. One is a tractor and the other a car' (she points to each vehicle in turn as she provides the name of each).
Ali looks up at her while she is speaking to him, then continues to roll the vehicles

back and forth in a straight line. Satti continues to watch. Ali makes the vehicles go in a circle and Satti responds.

Satti: 'Now the tractor is making a circle.'

Ali is encouraged by this and makes the car trace a circle on the carpet too.

Ali: (looks up and says in English) 'Car'.

Satti: 'Yes it is. Well done, Ali! It is a blue car.'

Ali continues to play and seems to enjoy making the vehicles start and stop. When he does this Satti says the appropriate word several times. Ali responds at times. He then looks up at Satti and gestures making an incline movement. Satti acknowledges what he's thinking and goes off for a few minutes returning with a ramp from a play set.

Satti: 'Look. A ramp.'

Ali is delighted and continues to move the vehicles up and down the ramp. Then he reaches over and gives Sati the car to play with.

And finally, what does this mean in implementing the EYFS successfully? From the revised framework itself and a growing body of evidence over more than a decade, we can identify pedagogical strategies that support young children's skills, knowledge and attitudes effectively. From this evidence a number of points emerge which we propose as our core principles through which to implement the new EYFS effectively:

- Use the EYFS framework to make learning relevant for all children.
- Ensure every child succeeds and set high expectations for each child.
- Start with first-hand experiences. Build on what children already know with structure and pace so they understand what is to be learned, as well as how and why.
- Recognize that babies and young children learn through their senses and movement and reflect that in your interactions with them.
- Balance play and more structured learning. Make judgements about the balance between activities led by children and those guided by adults.
- Make learning happen inside and outside the classroom. Make it real and relevant in stimulating and supporting environments.
- Encourage children to engage in learning at length and in depth.
- Organize your space to allow independence and choice so children develop learning skills, thinking skills and personal qualities for life.
- Use observation and formative assessment to inform what you do and what

you will do next with children. Reflect on the ways in which children learn as well as what they learn.

- Make children partners in their learning. Value partnerships with families and carers. Have a shared frame of reference between the setting, the child and his/her family.

Section review: Pedagogy in the EYFS

Thinking

The phrase 'use it or lose it' is often used in connection with using one's brain to think. What do you understand this means for babies and young children? What kinds of experiences would you recommend to build learning power to a parent of: i) a baby, ii) a two year old, iii) a five year old?

Reflecting

How do you promote learner involvement of the type described in the examples above? Consider the action points for your practice with reference to the work referred to earlier by Laevers and Moons.

Doing

Read *Building Learning Power* by Guy Claxton (footnote 15). In this book he talks about four learning domains of Resilience, Resourcefulness, Reciprocity and Reflection. How do these domains apply to young children's learning in the EYFS?

Conclusion

This chapter discussed two important and connected themes: how children learn and the approaches to teaching and interacting that best promote learning in the EYFS. We argued at the beginning of the chapter that learning takes place before a child is born through sensory learning and that learning continues to accelerate after birth. We discussed this with reference to key learning theories and principles. The growing brain is hard-wired to learn, pathways for learning are set early and form the basis of all future learning. To develop this, high quality learning experiences need to be provided at home, in settings and schools. The three characteristics of effective learning: playing and exploring, active learning and creating and thinking critically taken from the revised EYFS (2012) were explored and practical examples of each given to take this forward in the EYFS. In the final section we brought together research on how practitioners can support children's learning and presented a number of pedagogical strategies for readers to take forward into their own practice to implement the revised EYFS effectively and successfully.

Future Matters

Reaching this chapter is both the endpoint and beginning of a journey for us: we have explored the revised EYFS and what it is intended to achieve. We have also considered the conditions which support that achievement: play and playful teaching; interaction and sustained shared thinking; parents and home learning; the environment; school readiness, child development and policy, all of which will contribute to how effectively the EYFS will work in the various settings where it is put into practice. Our journey cannot be brought to its conclusion however without considering what will happen next, poised as we are on the edge of the future: the revised EYFS framework has been published; settings are beginning to respond to the 'new' framework and young children are beginning to make visits to schools – if they are old enough to be joining a reception class in September 2012; or to pre-schools and to nurseries if they are moving settings – this is the predictable rhythm of the year. The question we have is: 'Will anything be different?' If the answer is 'Not really' then the investment in a review of the EYFS has been wasted; if the answer is 'Yes, certainly!' then we would want to pose a second and even a third question: 'How will it be different?', 'What difference will the changes make?' Since it is impossible to predict what lies ahead, we can only say what we hope will happen and discuss what we think will matter most for young children both now and in the future.

Effects of the revised EYFS

The separation of the areas of learning and development into two discrete groups has the potential to make a massive impact on young children's early development, physically, emotionally and linguistically. In order to create that impact the ability of the workforce will be a contributing factor as will the degree to which parents are enabled to become involved in their children's learning. The recommendations from the Nutbrown Review[1] if accepted by the government will play a major role in shaping the future of the workforce. Indeed in shaping quality itself, since Professor Cathy Nutbrown states in her report: '*A new long-term vision is needed for the early years workforce, with a reformed system of qualifications to help achieve this. In working towards this vision, a balance must be struck between supporting existing good practice and challenging the sector to ensure provision is high quality in all settings'.* Within early years settings there is much existing good, even excellent practice – in places, where sometimes against the odds, people have a vision of what they believe is 'quality' for the children in their setting. Individual practitioners' beliefs and philosophies are, in our view, a strength of early years, truly reflecting the uniqueness of each setting and the diversity of children who attend them. At the same time there are still settings where the vision is either incomplete or unclear, where the needs of the organisation take precedence over those of the child – either because the leadership team lacks expertise in early years or because the quality of leadership is insufficiently robust for the onerous task of directing early years provision effectively.

Quality provision

So how can we ensure provision is high quality in all settings? An important step is to ensure that staff in early years settings are valued for the work they do and the expertise they have; another way is to ensure that the qualifications system equips practitioners *'with the knowledge and experience necessary for them to offer children high quality care and education, and to support professional development throughout their careers.'*[2] Without the benefit of excellent professional development it is unlikely that new entrants to the profession will be able to develop a personal vision, distinguishing what is important to them from what is not so important or that more established exponents will have the time to reflect on what they are doing, or to question why they are doing it.

Involving parents

Engaging parents in their children's learning requires that practitioners have the skills to be able to do that effectively and that parents are willing and able to be involved. The newly published eight page *Parents' Guide to the Early Years Foundation Stage Framework*[3] devotes one page to informing parents how to support their child's learning, for example, suggesting that on a trip to the supermarket parents talk to their child about 'all the different packaging shapes' or about 'what you are doing that day'. This is what most parents or their substitutes such as carers or grandparents do as a matter of course. The challenge isn't about what the many do but about what the few may not do; those parents who do not have the capacity whether a one or two parent working family or those families on the margins who struggle to face mornings because of problems linked to stressors such as mental health, domestic violence or poverty. Engaging these parents will involve the greatest struggle yet deliver the greatest prize. Many children's centres and schools are working together or separately to successfully achieve this – through a long-haul approach based on building the trust and confidence of those parents whose comfort zone ends when they encounter schools or 'official' buildings.

Parents themselves are often the best ambassadors for engaging other parents and in some local authorities such as Knowsley, where as part of a 'Radical efficiency initiative': *'They realised that their work needed to empower families to support themselves – that this was the key to behaviour change'*[4] such changes are beginning to be developed reflecting *'ideas for transforming early years that are aimed at building social capacity and effecting a radical transformation of the children's centres' role as a hub for community activities. This transformation will include a **parents' social network**, volunteers and a **community fund for social enterprise** but the challenge is to place these within coherent and sustainable parent-led governance'.*[5] The likely outcome from such a process is parents who are empowered to understand how to give their children a better chance in life and who recognise that the everyday things they do with and for their children will contribute to securing their children's success.

Regulation and inspection

Another area worthy of debate is the role of regulation and inspection. As we move forward we know that Ofsted is proposing to step back from an enforcement model in order to establish a self-evaluative approach. We heartily support this proposal since we believe that one of the confusions for leaders and managers has often been around a lack of autonomy or decision-making in the process. This has not been helpful and, a little like imposed discipline, does not encourage the recalcitrant child to improve their behaviour – merely to endeavour not to get caught! So we look forward to a future where Ofsted inspections are about providers and inspectors sharing a vision of what is best for children in a respectful process which retains the rigour in terms of safety and welfare but which recognises that the 'how' of what happens in settings is the outcome of a vision which has been developed by educators who understand the 'spirit' of the EYFS: children, their development, pedagogy and play. This is culture with a small 'c' which embraces these children, in this place, at this time and it is created by educators who are in tune with their own emotions, their own philosophy, the ethos of the setting and their beliefs about what young children are like and how they learn.

Child development

When the curriculum is in the hands of such experts we can assume that what is on offer is focused on children's needs and interests and that 'outcomes', 'standards' and 'school readiness' are placed appropriately in the taxonomy of what is important. Clearly they are important; we would be foolish to assume otherwise having argued at the start of this book that policy matters in the early years. However child development is imperative too and what is most essential is that children should emerge from their early years as enthusiastic, motivated, interested and keen to learn as they were when they first walked through the door that had the words Early Years Foundation Stage written above it, whether they were three months old or three years old. We believe that the early years are important in their own right – simply because these are the years when children find a self; find a voice and find their feet. The strength of the self is contingent on the strengths of early relationships – through parents and family members first and the key person when the child attends an EYFS setting. The child's voice is strengthened when it is heard and the child's views acknowledged, whether they are a baby swiping the spoon away from their lips or a four year old firmly sticking to their decision to wear a party outfit on an 'ordinary' day. Finding our feet is something we all do in transition reaching at some point the state of feeling fully confident so that we can put our feet 'under the table'. The use of this analogy is helpful because 'finding one's feet' is both a literal act in early childhood at the same time as a metaphorical position which describes self-confidence. Confident children usually become confident people. Confident people enjoy greater success and happiness than those lacking in self-esteem. Confidence comes from many sources: from environments that enable the child to feel competent; from positive relationships that reflect back to the child that they are accepted and valued and from learning through which the child feels a sense of agency and a desire to find out and to learn more.

Learning and development in the early years are closely connected and for the youngest children the two are barely differentiated, but as children mature their learning will be focused increasingly on the specific areas: Literacy, Mathematics, Understanding the World and Expressive Arts and Design. If children's experiences in the EYFS are to enable them to be their best selves then learning in each of these areas will be important – as we indicated at the beginning of this volume. Reading and writing will continue to be necessary skills notwithstanding the increasing range of technology options such as emoticons available as 'apps' for phones and the increasing use of mobile phones and 'skyping' to convey the spoken word in conversations between people physically at a distance from one another. Similarly a rise in the quantity and use of information technology will mean that babies and young children increasingly become 'tool-users' of this technological era. As we have indicated throughout this book technology is here to stay and every pre-school and early years school setting has electronic devices. The key will be to balance or offset some of these devices with the dependable materials that children have played with and in for aeons: water, mud, earth, sand, clay, stones, twigs, these are the things of childhood that are in danger of rapidly disappearing, the contents of the treasure chest of the natural world.

Ideal provision

So, in conclusion what do we hope will emerge as a new group of children begin life and learning in the revised EYFS from September 2012? Let us assume we are thinking about a baby who has been visiting a setting for several months. By September 2012 she is ready to start attending daily as her mother returns to work – what will be most important for her? Our baby will need to have established a bond with her key person who will play a role in her daily care; she will need to have lots of reminders of home and the important people she has left there, this might include pictures of family members or pets and things that smell of home, such as a scarf. As well as these she may be able to listen to the comforting sound of her mother's voice (or other family members' voices) recorded in a sound box, either speaking or singing a lullaby. Her day will be made into manageable chunks that become predictable and enjoyable because she is listened to and her voice is heard. As this routine becomes established the pattern of the day will be shared with her through a timetable. The setting will feel like a 'home from home' and she will be relaxed and confident because she is emotionally and physically 'contained'. In this context she is able to play and explore, to be active and to learn. The environment will offer her many contexts for learning: the long grass to hide in, puddles to splash in, books and songs to wallow in and most of all other children and people to share her journey in an exchange of words and laughter and delight. In such a context she will be enabled to be her 'best self'; that is a wish for all children in the EYFS whoever they are and wherever they experience it.

Challenges ahead

The challenge we all face is to ensure the principles of the EYFS are retained so that early education is right for every child. The way we can do this is through valuing the incredibly good work that goes on daily throughout EYFS settings, celebrating it and recognising those settings, leaders, managers and practitioners who make a difference to children's lives, by being 'there' for children, understanding them, believing in them and wanting the best for them. That is the majority; there is no room for complacency however and the minority who do not achieve such heights may, like children, need a helping hand to guide them to become their best. Ultimately we are all responsible for making early education better for young children – it is essential that each of us continues to finds ways to share what we know is good about early years education and to continually build on what we know to make the future better than ever for our children and our children's children. Children are our future – the future really matters.

References and Bibliography

Introduction

1   Nutbrown, Cathy. (2012) *Interim Review of Early Education And Childcare Qualifications*: Interim Report: Review of Early Education and Childcare Qualifications

Chapter 1

1   DFE (2012) *Statutory Framework for the Early Years Foundation Stage* March 2012

2   Ibid

3   DfEE/QCA (2000) *Curriculum Guidance for the Foundation Stage*, QCA Publications

4   DfES (2002*) Birth to Three Matters* Sure Start/DfES

5   *National Standards for Under Eights Daycare & Childminding* (2003) DfES & DWP, Nottingham

6   DfES (2007) *Statutory Framework for the Early Years Foundation Stage*, DfES Publications, Nottingham

7   http://www.thefreedictionary.com/neuroscience

8   Wismer, A.B. & Polak, S.D. in 'Emotion Processing and the Developing Brain' in *Human behaviour, learning and the developing brain: Typical development* Edited by Donna Coch, Kurt, W. Fischer and Geraldine Dawson 2007, The Guilford Press, New York

9   Ibid

10 'Brain Mechanisms and Early Learning' (2001) Neville, H. reported in First High Level Forum: Learning Sciences and Brain Research: Potential Implications for Education Policies and Practices, Sackler Institute, New York City OECD-CERI

11 Ibid

12 HM Government/Field, F. (2010) The Foundation Years: Preventing poor children becoming poor adults, The report of the Independent Review on Poverty and Life Chances; Allen, G. (MP) (2011) Early Intervention: The Next Steps, An Independent Report to Her Majesty's Government; Heckman. James,

J. (2011) The American Family in Black & White: A Post-Racial Strategy for Improving Skills to Promote Equality, Daedalus (accessed on the internet)

13 Currie, J. PhD,Economic Impact of Head Start, University of California, USA (Published online 16 December 2005)

14 http://www.nhsa.org/files/static_page_files/0610CCDD-1D09-3519-ADAF419AF96C38E0/Head_Start_Return_On_Investment_Brief_LAS-yv.pdf accessed on 11th January 2012

15 http://www.independent.co.uk/news/obituaries/norman-glass-civil-servant-whose-work-led-to-the-sure-start-programme-1774008.html

16 http://news.bbc.co.uk/1/hi/education/382986.stm

17 QCA/DCSF (2008) Early Years Foundation Stage Profile Handbook, Piccadilly, London

18 DFE (2011) Statistical First Release SFR 28/2011 (internet source)

19 Crawford, C., Dearden, L. & Greaves, E. (2011) Does when you are born matter? Institute for Fiscal Studies & Nuffield Foundation

20 Leon Feinstein 2003 accessed online on 120112 at: http://cep.lse.ac.uk/centrepiece/v08i2/feinstein.pdf

21 http://www.guardian.co.uk/education/2011/jun/14/poor-children-research-innate-intelligence? CMP=twt_gu

22 Allen, G. (MP) Early Intervention, The Next Steps, Early years, life chances and equality: a literature review 2008 Equality & Human Rights Commission,

23 Johnson, Paul & Kossykh, Yulia (2008) Early years, life chances and equality: a literature review Equality & Human Rights Commission, Frontier Economics

24 HM Government; Allen, G. (MP) (2011), Opening Doors, Breaking Barriers: A Strategy for Social Mobility Early Intervention, Smart Investment, Massive Savings; A New Approach to Child Poverty: Tackling the Causes of Disadvantage and Transforming Families' Lives, DWP/DoE

25 DFE/DoH *Families in the Foundation Years Evidence Pack*, (July 2011)

26 Ibid

27 Heckman, James.J. (May 2011) Creating a More Equal and Productive Britain a lecture for the Young Foundation and the Studio Schools Trust Centre for Economic Performance, London School of Economics

28 Robert Lynch (2005) Policy Perspectives: Early Childhood Investment Yields Big Pay Off, WestEd, San Francisco, California

29 Heckman

30 Heckman, James, J. (2011) Creating a More Equal and Productive Britain a

lecture for the Young Foundation and the Studio Schools Trust Centre for Economic Performance, London School of Economics

31 DFE (2011) Early Years Foundation Stage Consultation Draft Document 6 July

32 Ibid

33 DFE (2011) Early Years Foundation Stage Consultation Draft Document 6 July

34 UNICEF (2008) Getting Ready for School: A Child-to-Child Approach School Readiness Framework

35 Ibid

36 Bruce, T. (1991) Early Childhood Education (Seventh Impression) Hodder & Stoughton, London

37 Ibid

38 DFE Research Report (June 2011) Performing against the odds: developmental trajectories of children in the EPPSE 3–16 study: Iram Siraj-Blatchford, Aziza Mayo, Edward Melhuish, Brenda Taggart, Pam Sammons & Kathy Sylva

39 OECD (2007) Understanding the Brain: The Birth of a Learning Science

40 Early Childhood Highlights (2000) Volume 1 Issue 3

41 NAEYC (1995) School Readiness Position Statement

42 Dame Clare Tickell (2011) *The Early Years: Foundations for life, health and learning, An Independent Report on the Early Years Foundation Stage to Her Majesty's Government*

43 National Scientific Council on the Developing Child (2007) The Science of Early Childhood Development: Closing the Gap Between What We Know and What We Do

44 Hawley, T & Gunner, M. (2000) *Starting Smart How Early Experiences Affect Brain Development* Zero to Three

45 UN Convention on the Rights of the Child

46 Nutbrown, Cathy. (2012) *Interim Review of Early Education And Childcare Qualifications*: Interim Report: Review of Early Education and Childcare Qualifications

47 Ibid

Chapter 2

1 DoE/Early Education (2012) *Development Matters in the Early Years Foundation Stage*, London

2 Dame Clare Tickell (2011) *The Early Years: Foundations for life, health and*

learning, An Independent Report on the Early Years Foundation Stage to Her Majesty's Government

3   DFE (2012) *Statutory Framework for the Early Years Foundation Stage* March 2012

4   Ibid

5   DoE/Early Education (2012) *Development Matters in the Early Years Foundation Stage*, London

6   Elman et al, 1996

7   Bronfenbrenner, U. (1989). Ecological systems theory. In R. Vasta (ed), *Annals of child development. Vol. 6, pp.187–249.* Boston, MA: JAI Press, Inc.

8   Evangelou, M. et al. (2009). *Early Years Learning and Development Literature Review.* Research Report DCSF-RR176. London: DCSF

9   In Brief: The Science of Early Childhood Development Centre on the Developing Child: Harvard University accessed at www.developingchild.harvard.edu

10 Doherty, J. & Hughes, M. (2009). *Child Development. Theory and Practice 0–11.* Essex. Pearson Education

11 Rice, D. & Barone, S., Jr. (2000). Critical periods of vulnerability for the developing nervous system: evidence from humans and animal models. *Environmental Health Perspectives*, 108(Suppl. 3), 511–533

12 Shonkoff, J.P & Garner, A.S. (2012). 'The Lifelong Effects of Early Childhood Adversity and Toxic Stress'. *Pediatrics* Vol. 129 No. 1 January

13 National Scientific Council on the Developing Child (2007a)

14 Early Intervention – The Next Steps An Independent Report to Her Majesty's Government Graham Allen MP January 2011

15 Department of Health (2011) *Health Visitor Implementation Plan 2011–15 A Call to Action. London: DH. page 7*

16 *The Timing and Quality of Early Experiences Combine to Shape Brain Architecture: Working Paper #5.* December 2007. Center on the Developing Child at Harvard University: NSCDC

17 Ibid

18 DoE (2012) Development Matters in the Early Years Foundation Stage, London

19 DFE (2011) Support and aspiration: A new approach to special educational needs and disability – A consultation

20 DFE (2012) *Statutory Framework for the Early Years Foundation Stage* March 2012

21 L. Gandini & G. Forman (eds). *The Hundred Languages of Children.* Norwood, NJ: Ablex.

22 Marmot, M. (2010). *Fair Society, Healthy Lives. The Marmot Review. Strategic review of health inequalities in England post-2010*. London: The Marmot Review.

23 DFE (2012) *Statutory Framework for the Early Years Foundation Stage* March 2012

24 DFE (2011) Support and aspiration: A new approach to special educational needs and disability – A consultation

Chapter 3

1 Dame Clare Tickell (2011) The Early Years: Foundations for life, health and learning, An Independent Report on the Early Years Foundation Stage to Her Majesty's Government

2 National Scientific Council on the Developing Child (2007) The Science of Early Childhood Development: Closing the Gap Between What We Know and What We Do

3 OECD 2007 Understanding the Brain: The Birth of a Learning Science 4

4 Ibid

5 Ibid

6 Dame Clare Tickell (2011) The Early Years: Foundations for life, health and learning, An Independent Report on the Early Years Foundation Stage to Her Majesty's Government

7 Hall, John. (2005) A review of the contribution of brain science to teaching and learning

8 Ibid

9 Ibid

10 DFE (2012) Statutory Framework for the Early Years Foundation Stage March 2012

11 Ibid

12 Ibid

Chapter 4

1 Californian Infant and Toddler Learning and Development Foundations 2009

2 *Understanding the Brain: the Birth of a Learning Science New insights on learning through cognitive and brain science* accessed on 13 February 2012 at http://www.oecd.org/dataoecd/39/53/40554190.pdf

3 ICAN Talk Series Issue 7

4 http://health.usnews.com/health-news/family-health/childrens-health/

articles/2009/10/21/prolonged-use-of-pacifier-linked-to-speech-problems accessed 14 February 2012

5   ICAN Talk Series Issue 7

6   National Literacy Trust Early Language Development: A review of the Evidence from Birth to Age Three www.literacytrust.org.uk

7   Betty Hart, Ph.D. and Todd R. Risley, Ph.D.(1995) *Meaningful Differences in the Everyday Experience of Young American Children* Brookes Publishing Company

8   Paterson, C. (2011) *Parenting Matters: Early Years and Social Mobility*, CentreForum *in Pre-school: Talking, Reading and Writing.* Newark, DE International Reading Association

9   Roskos, K.A., Tabors, P.O. & Lenhart, L.A. Oral Language and Early Literacy in Pre-school: Talking, Reading and Writing. Newark, DE International Reading Association.

10 New York State PreKindergarten Guidelines http://www.p12.nysed.gov/ciai/common_core_standards/pdfdocs/nyslsprek.pdf

11 Applied Lingusitics accessed at http://www.slideshare.net/petitlutin/applied-linguistics-1class-1 on 8 March 2012

12 Walmsley, S. (2008) *Closing the Circle*, San Francisco: Jossey Bass

13 Ibid

14 Center on the Developing Child at Harvard University (2007). A Science-Based Framework for Early Childhood Policy: Using Evidence to Improve Outcomes in Learning, Behavior, and Health for Vulnerable Children

15 *Early Intervention – The Next Steps* An Independent Report to Her Majesty's Government Graham Allen MP January 2011

16 Desforges, Charles & Abouchaar, Alberto The Impact of Parental Involvement, Parental Support and Family Education on Pupil Achievements and Adjustment: A Literature Review. DfES Research Report 433

17 Leavitt R. L. Power and Sensitivity in Infant-Toddler Care 1994 State University of New York

18 Cohen et al 2005 Helping Young Children Succeed: Strategies to Promote Early Childhood Social and Emotional Development; Zero to Three

19 http://searchcio.techtarget.com/definition/soft-skills accessed on 9 March 2012

20 DFE (2010) Statutory Framework for the Early Years Foundation Stage (March 2012)

21 Ibid

22 Joseph, G. & Strain, P.sS. 2003 Comprehensive evidence-based social-emotional

curricular for young children: An analysis of efficacious adoption potential. Topics in Early Childhood Special Education, 23 (2):65–76.

23 WAVE Report: Violence and What To Do About It, 2005

24 Holmes, J. John Bowlby and Attachment Theory1993 Routledge London and New York.

25 Ibid

26 Siegel, D.J *The Developing Mind* 1999 The Guilford Press, New York

27 *Mental health promotion and mental illness prevention: The economic case* Martin Knapp, David McDaid, & Michael Parsonage (editors) Personal, Social Services Research Unit, London School of Economics and Political Science April 2011 Report published by the DOH, London

28 OFSTED 2008 TellUs3 National Report

29 *Mental health promotion and mental illness prevention: The economic case* Martin Knapp, David McDaid, & Michael Parsonage (editors) Personal, Social Services Research Unit, London School of Economics and Political Science April 2011 Report published by the DOH, London

30 Raver, C. C. (2002). Emotions matter: Making the case for the role of young children's emotional development for early school readiness. *Social Policy Report,* *16*(3), 3–19.

31 DEF (2012) *Statutory Framework for the Early Years Foundation Stage* March 2012

32 Goddard-Blythe, S. (2005) *The Well-Balanced Child* Hawthorn Press

33 Deacon, C. 2010 *Boost Your Baby's Development* Hodder Education

34 http://medical-dictionary.thefreedictionary.com/pincer+grasp

35 New York State Prekindergarten Foundation for the Common Core

36 Eliot L. *What's Going on in There?* 2000 Bantam New York

37 DOH (2011) *Start Active Stay Active A report on physical activity for health from the four home countries'* Chief Medical Officers

38 DFE (2010) *Statutory Framework for the Early Years Foundation Stage* March 2012

39 Ibid

40 Holmes, J. *John Bowlby and Attachment Theory* 1993 Routledge, London and New York

Chapter 5

1   World Literacy Foundation (2012) The Economic & Social Cost of Illiteracy: *A snapshot of illiteracy and its causes in the UK and a global context* Interim Report from the World Literacy Foundation

2   Every Child A Chance Trust (2009) *The Long Term Costs of Numeracy Difficulties*, Every Child A Chance Trust

3   Centre for Social Justice Report/Adele Eastman (2011) *No excuses: A review of educational exclusion* A policy report by the Centre for Social Justice

4   Jama, Deeqa. & Dugdale, George. (2010) *Literacy: State of the Nation: A picture of Literacy in the UK today*National Literacy Trust

5   *The Importance of Phonics: Securing Confident Reading* accessed on 26 March 2012   @   http://media.education.gov.uk/assets/files/pdf/p/learning%20to%20 read%20through%20phonics%20%20%20information%20for%20parents.pdf

6   Ibid

7   Ibid

8   Ofsted (2011) 'Getting them reading early': Distance learning materials for inspecting reading within the new framework

9   Rose, J. (2006) *Independent Review of the Teaching of Early Reading Final Report (DfES)*

10 DFE (2012) Statutory Framework for the Early Years Foundation Stage March 2012

11 Rose, J. (2006) *Independent Review of the Teaching of Early Reading Final Report (DfES)*

12 http://www.yourdictionary.com/reading accessed online 26 March 2012

13 DFE (2012) Statutory Framework for the Early Years Foundation Stage March 2012

14 NYSED (2011) New York State Prekindergarten Foundation for the Common Core The New York State Education Department, Albany, New York 12234

15 Evangelou, M., Sylva, K. & Kyriacou, M. (2009) Early Years Learning and Development Literature Review, DfES

16 Workshop Trainer's Guide http://www.state.nj.us/education/ece/pd/lal/l4/guide. pdf

17 http://www.readingrockets.org/article/3408/

18 FfE (undated) Learning to read through phonics Information for parents parents (DoE website)

19 DFE *The Importance of Phonics: Securing Confident Reading* web accessed 26 March 2012

20 Rose, J. (2006) Independent Review of the Teaching of Early Reading Final Report, DfES

21 http://www.readingrockets.org/article/3408/

22 Harrison G. *Basic and Environmental Processes Underlying Writing Acquisition*, http://literacyencyclopedia.ca

23 Council for the Curriculum, Examinations and Assessment (Undated) *Language and Literacy in the Foundation Stage: Writing* accessed on 30 May 2012 http://www.nicurriculum.org.uk/docs/foundation_stage/areas_of_learning/language_and_literacy/LL_Writing.pdf

24 DfE (2012) Statutory *Framework for the Early Years Foundation Stage* March 2012

25 Rose, J. (2006) Independent Review of the Teaching of Early Reading Final Report, DfES.

26 Parsons, S. & Bynner, J. (2005) *Does Numeracy Matter More?* Published by the National Research and Development Centre for Adult Literacy and Numeracy

27 Ibid

28 Ginsburg, HP, Sun Lee, J and Stevenson Boyd, J (2008) *Mathematics Education for Young Children: What It is and How to Promote it* Social Policy Report, Volume XXII Number 1

29 Sarama, J and Clements, DH (2009) *Early Childhood Mathematics Education Research: Learning Trajectories for Young Children*, Routledge

30 Duncan et al (2007) in Ginsburg, HP, Sun Lee, J and Stevenson Boyd, J *Mathematics Education for Young Children: What It is and How to Promote it* Social Policy Report, Volume XXII Number 1, 2008

31 Sherman-LeVos, Jody L., PhD. (Published online 5 July 2010) 'Mathematics Instruction for Preschoolers', University of California, Berkeley, USA. In *Encyclopaedia on Early Childhood Development*

32 Ibid

33 Smith-Chant, B. (editor) (undated) *Acquisition of early numeracy: Key Messages* http://www.literacyencyclopedia.ca

34 Ginsburg, HP, Sun Lee, J and Stevenson Boyd, J (2008) *Mathematics Education for Young Children: What It is and How to Promote it* Social Policy Report, Volume XXII Number 1

35 Klibanoff, R. S., Levine, S. C., Huttenlocher, J., Vasilyeva, M., & Hedges, L. V. (2006). 'Preschool children's mathematical knowledge: The effect of teacher

'math talk". Developmental Psychology, 42(1), 59–69 in Ginsburg, HP, Sun Lee, J and Stevenson Boyd, J. (2008) *Mathematics Education for Young Children: What It is and How to Promote it* Social Policy Report, Volume XXII Number 1

36 DFE (2012) S*tatutory Framework for the Early Years Foundation Stage,* March 2012

37 DFE (2012) Statutory Fr*amework for the Early Years Foundation Stage* March 2012

38 Ibid

39 Ibid

40 Sarama, J and Clements,D.H. (2009) *Early Childhood Mathematics Education Research: Learning Trajectories for Young Children*, Routledge

41 Wright, B 1991 in Sarama, J and Clements,D.H. (2009) *Early Childhood Mathematics Education Research: Learning Trajectories for Young Children*, Routledge

42 Sarama, J and Clements,D.H. (2009) *Early Childhood Mathematics Education Research: Learning Trajectories for Young Children*, Routledge

43 Glasersfeld 1982 in ACER Research Conference 2000 Improving Numeracy Learning: What does the research tell us? Accessed at: http://www.acer.edu.au/documents/RC2000_Proceedings.pdf 30 May 2012

44 Sarama, J and Clements,D.H. (2009) *Early Childhood Mathematics Education Research: Learning Trajectories for Young Children*, Routledge

45 Ibid

46 NIH/National Institute of Child Health and Human Development (2012, June 27). Ability to estimate quantity increases in first 30 years of life. Science Daily. Retrieved July 30, 2012, from http://www.sciencedaily.com/releases/2012/06/120627103346.html

47 Ibid

48 Thomson, Ian. Visiting Professor at Northumbria University: *The principal counting principles* accessed online at https://www.ncetm.org.uk/public/files/712850/The+principal+counting+principles.pdf

49 Ibid

50 Evangelou, M., Sylva, K. & Kyriacou, M. (2009) *Early Years Learning and Development Literature Review*, DfES

51 Ofsted (2012) Subsidiary Guidance: *Supporting the inspection of maintained schools and academies* from January 2012

52 Sarama,, J and Clements,D.H. (2009) Early Childhood Mathematics Education Research: Learning Trajectories for Young Children, Routledge

53 DFE (2012) *Statutory Framework for the Early Years Foundation Stage* March 2012

54 Gopnik, A. (2009) Journal Title: Zero to Three Volume 30 (2) ps 28–32 Reading Minds: How Infants Come to Understand Others

55 DFE (2012) *Statutory Framework for the Early Years Foundation Stage* March 2012

56 Ibid

57 Ibid

58 Gutnick, A.L, Robb, M, Takeuchi, L and Kotler, J. (2010) *Always Connected: The New Media Habits of Young Children*. New York: The Joan Ganz Cooney Center at Sesame Workshop

59 Ibid

60 The Guardian Weekend (2011): Mum, can I play with the iPad?19 November 2011

61 Woolridge, M. B. (2012) Playing with Technology: Mother-Toddler Interaction and Toys with Batteries (A thesis submitted in partial fulfilment of the requirements for the MA; The University of British Columbia (Vancouver) April 2010) accessed on 30 April 2012 https://circle.ubc.ca/bitstream/handle/2429/23711/ubc_2010_spring_woolridge_michaela.pdf?sequence=1

62 Computing at School Working Group http://www.computingatschool.org.uk

63 NAACE (2012) Draft Framework for Information and Communication Technology (ICT) Early Years Foundation Stage, Key Stage 1, Key Stage 2, March 2012

64 Ibid

65 DFE (2012) *Statutory Framework for the Early Years Foundation Stage* March 2012

66 NAACE (2012) Draft Framework for Information and Communication Technology (ICT) Early Years Foundation Stage, Key Stage 1, Key Stage 2, March 2012

67 Robinson, K. (1999) *All Our Futures: Creativity, Culture and Education* Report to the Secretary of State for Education and Employment, the Secretary of State for Culture, Media and Sport, May 1999

68 DFE (2012) *Statutory Framework for the Early Years Foundation Stage* March 2012

69 HMIE (2006) *Emerging Good Practice in Promoting Creativity*

70 Malaguzzi, L. in Sharp, C. (2004) *Developing young children's creativity: what can we learn from research?* NFER

71 DFE (2012) *Statutory Framework for the Early Years Foundation Stage* March 2012

72 Sharp, C. (2004) *Developing Young Children's Creativity: what can we learn from research?* NFER

73 Robinson, K. (1999) *All Our Futures: Creativity, Culture and Education* Report to the Secretary of State for Education and Employment, the Secretary of State for Culture, Media and Sport, May 1999*

74 Yovanka B. Lobo and Adam Winsler (2006) *The Effects of a Creative Dance and Movement Program on the Social Competence of Head Start Preschoolers* George Mason University Blackwell Publishing Ltd

75 Ibid

76 Sacha, Tori, J. and Russ, Sandra, W. *Effects of Pretend Imagery on Learning Dance in Preschool Children* Early Childhood Education Journal, Vol. 33, No. 5 (2006)

77 Bergen, D. (2002) *The Role of Pretend Play in Children's Cognitive Development* Miami University accessed on 1 June 2012 at: http://ecrp.uiuc.edu/v4n1/bergen.html

78 Meire, Johan (2006) *Qualitative Research on Children's Play*: A review of recent literature, Childhood and Society Research Centre, Belgium

Chapter 6

1 DFE (2102) *Statutory Framework for the Early Years Foundation Stage* March 2012

2 Ibid

3 Ibid

4 Ibid

5 Ibid

Chapter 7

1 Gordon, Gwen. (undated) What is Play? In search of a Universal Definition accessed at *www.gwengordonplay.com/pdf/what_is_play.pdf*Similar on 31st July 2012

2 Fagen, Robert (1981) Animal Play Behavior: New York: Viking

3 Smith, Peter, K. & Pellegrini, Anthony. (2008) *Learning Through Play* Published online in Encyclopaedia on Early Childhood Development

4   Ibid

5   Pellegrini, A., Dupuis, D. & Smith, Peter, K. (2006), *Play in Evolution and Development* Elsevier Inc

6   Hirsh-Pasek, Kathy. (PhD) & Golinkoff, Roberta, Michnick. (PhD) Why Play = Learning (Published online 15 October 2008) Encyclopedia on Early Childhood Development

7   Smith, Peter, K. & Pellegrini, Anthony. (Published online 2008) Learning Through Play, Encyclopaedia on Early Childhood Development

8   Dame Clare Tickell (2011) *The Early Years: Foundations for life, health and learning, An Independent Report on the Early Years Foundation Stage to Her Majesty's Government*

9   DFE (2011) *Early Years Foundation Stage Consultation Draft Document* 6 July

10 DFE (2011) Reforming the Early Years Foundation Stage (the EYFS): Government Response to consultation 20 December 2011

11 Ibid

12 DFE (2011) *Early Years Foundation Stage Consultation Draft Document* 6 July

13 DFE (2012) *Statutory Framework for the Early Years Foundation Stage* March 2012

14 Sutton-Smith, B. (2008) Play Theory American Journal of Play Summer 2008 accessed online Board of Trustees of the University of Illinois

15 Dame Clare Tickell (2011) *The Early Years: Foundations for life, health and learning, An Independent Report on the Early Years Foundation Stage to Her Majesty's Government*

16 Dewey, John. (1938), *Experience and Education.* New York: Kappa Delta Pi. Kindle Edition

17 Piaget, J. (1972) *Play, Dreams and Imitation in Childhood* Routledge and Kegan Paul, London

18 Hughes, Fergus P. (2010) *Children, Play and Development* 4th Edition, Sage

19 Almon, Joan. (undated) The Vital Role of Play in Childhood accessed on the web 3 January 2012 at: http://www.waldorfearlychildhood.org/article.asp?id=5

20 Rosenfeld, Alvin, M.D.(2004) From a talk at Rodeph Shalom School, New York, NY and sent to the Alliance by Dr. Rosenfeld on 27 February 2004 http://www.waldorfearlychildhood.org/article.asp?id=5.

21 Report of the Surgeon General's Conference on Children's Mental Health: A National Action Agenda 2000

22 Hirsh-Pasek, Kathy. &,Golinkoff, Roberta, Michnick. (PhD) 2008 *Why Play= Learning* Encyclopaedia on Early Childhood Development

23 Hirsh-Pasek, Kathy. Golinkoff, Roberta, Michnick., Berk, Laura E. & Singer. Dorothy (2009) *A Mandate for Playful Learning in Preschool: Presenting the Evidence*, Oxford University Press, New York

24 Ibid

25 Hughes, Fergus. P. (2010) Children, Play and Development 4th Edition, Sage

26 Sutton-Smith, B. (2008) Play Theory American Journal of Play Summer 2008 accessed online Board of Trustees of the University of Illinois

27 Hughes, Fergus. P. (2010) *Children, Play and Development* 4th Edition, Sage

28 Abbott, L & Langston, A. (2005) Birth to Three Matters: a framework to support children in their earliest years *European Early Childhood Education Research Journal*, 13, 1.

29 Ibid

30 Stone, S. J., & Stone W. *Symbolic Play and Emergent Literacy* International Council for Children's Play internet accessed http://www.iccp-play.org/documents/brno/stone1.pdf

31 Smith,Peter, K. & Pellegrini, Anthony. (2008) *Learning Through Play* Published online in Encyclopaedia on Early Childhood Development

32 Ibid

33 Stone, S. J., & Stone W. *Symbolic Play and Emergent Literacy* International Council for Children's Play internet accessed http://www.iccp-play.org/documents/brno/stone1.pdf

34 Ibid

35 Adding it Up: Helping Children Learn Mathematics (2001) edited by Kilpatrick, J., Swafford. J. J., & Findell, B. Washington DC: National Academy Press accessed at https://download.nap.edu/chapterlist.php?record_id=9822&type=pdf_chapter&free=1 on 3 January 2012

36 Seo, K.H. & Ginsburg H.P 'What is developmentally appropriate in early childhood mathematics education? Lessons from new research' in Hirsh-Pasek, Kathy. (PhD) & Golinkoff, Roberta, Michnick. (PhD) *Why Play = Learning* (published online 15 October 2008) Encyclopedia on Early Childhood Development.

37 DFE (2012) *Statutory Framework for the Early Years Foundation Stage* March 2012

38 Smith,Peter, K. & Pellegrini, Anthony. (2008) *Learning Through Play* Published online in Encyclopaedia on Early Childhood Development

39 Hirsh-Pasek, Kathy., Golinkoff, Roberta. Michnick., Berk, Laura. E. & Singer,

Dorothy. (2009) *A Mandate for Playful Learning in Preschool: Presenting the Evidence*, Oxford University Press, New York

Chapter 8

1 Lindon, J. (1998) *Understanding Child Development.* London: Thomson Learning
2 Bowlby, J, (1969) Attachment and loss. Vol 1: *Attachment.* New York: Basic
3 Newport, E.L. (1976) 'Motherese: The speech of mothers to young children'. In N. Castellan, D. Pisoni & G. Potts (eds), *Cognitive Theory.* Vol. 2. Hillsdale, NJ: Erlbaum
4 Ounce of Prevention Fund (2008). *Secure Attachment.* Chicago: OPF
5 Berk, L. (2006) *Child development.* Boston, MA: Allyn & Bacon. Page 320
6 Doherty, J. & Hughes, M. (2009). *Child Development. Theory and Practice 0–11.* Essex. Pearson Education
7 National Scientific Council on the Developing Child (2004). Working Paper No. 1. (Summer 2004).Young Children Develop in an Environment of Relationships. Harvard: NSCDC.
8 Roberts, R. (2002) *Self Esteem and Early Learning.* Second Edition. London: Paul Chapman Publishing pages.5–6
9 DFE (2012) *Statutory Framework for the Early Years Foundation Stage* March 2012
10 DoE/Early Education (2012) *Development Matters in the Early Years Foundation Stage*, London
11 DFE (2012) *Statutory Framework for the Early Years Foundation Stage* March 2012
12 Sroufe, A.L. (2005) 'Attachment and development: a prospective, longitudinal study from birth to adulthood', *Attachment and Human Development.* Vol. 7, page 365.
13 Ward, S. (2000). *Babytalk. The pioneering book that will change childcare forever.* London; The Random House Group.
14 Buckley, B. (2005) *Children's Communications Skills. From birth to five years. Abingdon, Oxon: Routledge.*
15 Siraj-Blatchford, I., Sylva, K., Muttock, S., Gilden,R. & Bell, D. (2002). *Researching Effective Pedagogy in the Early Years.* Research Report 356. London: DfES.
16 DCSF/National Strategies. (2008) *Every Child a Talker: Guidance for Early Language Lead Practitioners.* pp.41–42. Nottingham: DCSF Publications

17   Fleet, M. (1995) quoted in Dunkin, D. & Hanna, P. (1995). *Thinking Together, Quality Adult: Child Interactions* NZCER

18   Wolf, M. (2000) *Proust and the Squid. The story and science of the reading brain.* Thriplow, Cambridge: Icon Books Ltd. page 20.

19   Childers, J. B., & Tomasello, M. (2002). 'Two-year olds learn novel nouns, verbs and conventional actions from massed or distributed exposures'. D*evelopmental Psychology,* 38(6), 867–978.

Chapter 9

1   DFE (2012) *Statutory Framework for the Early Years Foundation Stage* March 2012

2   The Plowden Report (1967) Children and their Primary Schools A Report of the Central Advisory Council for Education (England) *London: Her Majesty's Stationery Office 1967*

3   Dame Clare Tickell (2011) *The Early Years: Foundations for life, health and learning, An Independent Report on the Early Years Foundation Stage to Her Majesty's Government*

4   Evangelou, E. & Sylva, K. (2003) *The Effects of the Peers Early Educational Partnership (PEEP) on Children's Developmental Progress.* Research Report.489. University of Oxford.

5   Ofsted (2009) Family learning. An evaluation of the benefits of family learning for participants, their families and the wider community.

6   *Early Intervention – The Next Steps* An Independent Report to Her Majesty's Government Graham Allen MP January 2011

7   www.foundation years.org.uk

8   Grandparent Care Briefing Paper June Statham November (2011)

9   DFE website. Press Notice 16 October 2011

10   Learning and Teaching Scotland (2010) *Pre-Birth to Three: Positive Outcomes for Scotland's Children and Families. National Guidance. Partnership Working. Glasgow:* Learning and Teaching Scotland.

11   Lewis, J. et al. (2008). Patterns of paid and unpaid work in Western Europe: gender, commodification, preferences and the implications for policy. *Journal of European and Social Policy.*

12   *How primary and secondary schools help parents and carers to improve their child's learning* (DCSF, 2009)

13   Supporting parents with their children's 'at home' learning and development. A guide for practitioners (DCSF, 2009)

14 Laurie Day, Jenny Williams and Jackie Fox (2009) Supporting parents with their children's 'at home' learning and development Research Report

15 http://parentview.ofsted.gov.uk/

16 Paterson, C. (2011). *Parenting Matters: early years and social mobility.* London: CentreForum

17 Feinstein, L. & Sabates, R. (2006) '*Does Education have an impact on mothers' educational attitudes and behaviours'* DfES Research Brief RCB01–06. London: DCSF

18 Desforges, C. & Abouchaar, A. (2003). *The impact of parental involvement, parental support and family education on pupil achievement and adjustment: A literature review.* London: DfES

19 Evangelou, M., Sylva, K., Kyriacou, M., Wild, M. & Glenny, G. (2009). *Early Years Learning and Development Literature Review.* Research Report DCSF-RR176. London: DCSF

20 National Literacy Trust (2011). *A research review: the importance of families and the home environment,* Angelica Bonci (2008, revised 2010 and March 2011)

21 Sylva, K., Melhuish, E., Sammons, P., Siraj-Blatchford, I., Taggart, B. & Elliot, K. (2003). *The Effective Provision of Pre-School Education (EPPE) Project: Findings from the Pre-School Period.* London: IOE.

22 Family and Parenting Institute (2009). *Health Visitors: a progress report*; based on a March 2007 YouGov poll of parents with children aged under 5. April.

23 Lugo-Gill, J. & Tamis-LeMonda, C. (2008). 'Family Resources and Parenting Quality: Links to Children's Cognitive Development across the First 3 years'. *Child Development*, 79, 1065–1085

24 Melhuish E., Belsky J., Macpherson K., Cullis A. (2010) *National Evaluation of Sure Start: Quality of Childcare centres used by 3–4 year old children in Sure Start areas and the relationship with child outcomes.* London: Birkbeck.

25 Feinstein, L., & Symons, J. (1999). Attainment in secondary school. *Oxford Economic Papers*

26 Sammons, P., Sylva, K., Melhuish, E., Siraj-Blatchford, I., Taggart, B. Barreau, S. &. Grabbe,Y. (2007). 'Influences on Children's Development and Progress in Key Stage 2: Social /behavioural outcomes in Year 5', London: DCSF Research Report No. DCSF-RR007

27 Denton, K., West, J., & Walston, J. (2003). *Reading – Young children's achievement and classroom experiences.* Washington, DC: U.S. Dept. of Education

28 Parents' Guide to the Early Years Foundation Stage Framework (4children) (2012)

29 http://www.oakwood.herts.sch.uk/downloads/learning_workshop_may11.pdf

Chapter 10

1   DoE/Early Education (2012) *Development Matters in the Early Years Foundation Stage*, London

2   Gopnik, A., Meltzoff, A. & Kuhl, P. (1999) *How Babies Think*. London: Weidenfeld & Nicolson.

3   Pascal, C. and Bertram, T. (1997) In *Researching Early Childhood 3*, Settings in Interaction. Goteborg University, Early Childhood Research and Development Centre.

4   Flavell, J.H, et al. (2002). *Cognitive development*. Upper Saddle River, NJ: Prentice-Hall.

5   Siegler, R.S & Alibali, M.W. (2005) Children's Thinking. Upper Saddle River, NJ: Prentice Hall.

6   Case, R. (1998) The Development of Conceptual Structures. In W. Damon (Series ed.) & D. Kuhn & R.S. Siegler (Vol. eds), *Handbook of child psychology: Vol. 2, Cognition, perception, and language*. New York: Wiley.

7   Vygotsky, L.S. (1978) *Mind in Society: The Development of Higher Psychological Processes*. Cambridge, MA: Harvard University Press.

8   Brainerd, C.J. & Reyna, V.F. (1993) Mere memory testing creates false memories in children. *Developmental Psychology*, 32, pp.467–78

9   Radin, J.P (2009) Brain-compatible teaching and learning. Implications for teacher education. *Education Horizons*, 88 (1).

10 Aamodt, S. & Wang, S. (2011) *Welcome to your child's brain from utero to uni..* Oxford: Oneworld Publications.

11 Laevers, F. (1994). The innovative project Experiential Education and the definition of quality in education. In: Laevers F. (Ed.). *Defining and assessing quality in early childhood education*. Studia Paedagogica. Leuven, Leuven University Press, pp. 159–172.

12 *Ofsted (2010) Learning: creative approaches that raise standards. Manchester: Ofsted.*

13 Athey. C (1990) *Extending Thought in Young Children*, London: PCP

14 Carr, M. (2001) *Assessment in Early Childhood Settings: Learning Stories*. London: Paul Chapman Publishing.

15 Claxton, G. (2002) *Building Learning Power*. Bristol: TLO Limited.

16 Dweck, C. (2006) Mindset: *The New Psychology of Success*. Random House.

17 Evangelou, M., Sylva, K., Kyriacou, M., Wild, M. & Glenny, G. (2009). *Early Years Learning and Development Literature Review*. Research Report DCSF-RR176. London: DCSF, page 23.

18 DoE/Early Education (2012) *Development Matters in the Early Years Foundation Stage*, London

19 Shackell, A., Butler,N., Doyle, P. & Ball, D. (2008) *Design for Play: A guide to creating successful play spaces.* Nottingham: DCMS/DCSF Publications

20 Johnston, J. (2004) The value of exploration and discovery. *Primary Science Review 85* November/December

21 OECD (2004). *Curricula and Pedagogies in Early Childhood Education and Care Five curriculum outlines.* Paris: OECD

22 Riley, J. (2007) The child, the context and early childhood education. In J. Riley (ed). *Learning in the Early Years.* London: Sage

23 Siraj-Blatchford et al., 2002, REPEY, p.28.

24 Play Research Seminar. Leeds Metropolitan University, Leeds.

25 Learning, Playing and Interacting, 2009, p.15

26 Siraj-Blatchford et al., (2002). Researching Effective Pedagogy in the Early Years (REPEY) Document 421 Vignette 8)

Chapter 11

1 Nutbrown, Cathy. (2012) *Interim Review of Early Education And Childcare Qualifications*: Interim Report: Review of Early Education and Childcare Qualifications

2 Ibid

3 DFE (2012) *Parents' Guide to the Early Years Foundation Stage* Crown Copyright 2012 accessed on the internet 28 June 2012

4 NESTA (Undated) *Radical Efficiency in Early Years Settings: Community Co-Production in Knowsley*, Innovations Unit/NESTA accessed online at http://www.nesta.org.uk/library/documents/TEYVisualCaseStudyKnowsley.pdf

5 Ibid